BICYCLING
The Colorado Rockies

BICYCLING
The Colorado Rockies

Vici De Haan

PRUETT **P** PUBLISHING COMPANY
Boulder, Colorado

First Edition
1 2 3 4 5 6 7 8 9

Printed in the United States of America
Library of Congress Cataloging in Publication Data

De Haan, Vici.
  Bicycling the Colorado Rockies.

  Bibliography: p.
    1. Bicycle touring—Rocky Mountains—Guide-books.
2. Rocky Mountains—Description and travel—Guide-
books. I. Title.
GV1045.5.R6D4   917.8′0433   82-423
ISBN 0-87108-615-8   AACR2

Acknowledgements

Many thanks to Warren De Haan, my favorite touring companion, for accompanying me on these beautiful mountain rides. Also thanks to Dave Rearick and Julie Inwood for their efforts in proofing the manuscript. Without their help, this job would have been even more difficult.

Preface

Riding in the Colorado Rockies can be one of the most exhilarating experiences imaginable! Here you can avoid much of the heat of the plains as well as come into close contact with the many moods of nature.

As I researched the routes, I looked for historical places to visit along with possible hiking trails. My own bicycle touring has been done in two ways: some days I would ride a route with my only objective being to get from one point to another with occasional stops along the way. On other days, I would plan to arrive at a particular point where I planned to stay for a few days to enjoy some local bike rides, hiking the nearby trails, or visiting the historical sites. As both an avid bicyclist and hiker, I have found the trip was more enjoyable when I broke it up to take advantage of the various options offered by a particular spot.

Contents

General Information

HIKING

Most of the hikes will not require any additional equipment from what I would ordinarily have for my bicycling. I always carry an extra quart canteen for water and a small nylon backpack for my lunch and rain gear. Unless the trail is still snow-covered, tennis shoes are generally adequate footgear. A small collapsible hat will also add to your hiking comfort.

CAMPING

Most towns have campgrounds available: both commercial and some provided by the National Forest Service. The commercial campgrounds generally provide showers and a small grocery store. The forest service campgrounds usually have picnic tables, pit toilets and drinking water. However, water wasn't always available in all the campgrounds, depending upon the time of the year you're there, so I would advise asking about its availability before going to the work of setting up camp.

ACCOMMODATIONS

Whenever possible, I have included a good sampling of the motels and hotels available. I have included telephone numbers when I was able to get them, so you can call ahead to make any desired reservations. When a town is large, generally no reservation is necessary, but when it's more remote or small, reservations are suggested. I often waited to call ahead on the morning for which I needed the reservation.

EATING

I have found that some bicyclists prefer to pick up picnic supplies along the way for their noon meal, while others like to eat out in a cafe. For this reason, I've kept a running log while riding the various routes of some restaurants and grocery stores along the way, along with suggestions for picnic spots.

BIKE SHOPS

Whenever I could find them, I have included the names of bike shops in the various towns.

TOURIST ATTRACTIONS

As I toured the state, I stopped at numerous Chambers of Commerce to collect information on the area. I have included as much of this as I felt was feasible in my ride descriptions, but have not included any actual entrance fees, since these fluctuate from year to year. Often a town offered very little in the way of side attractions, while others were full. I found it helpful to know about an area in advance so I could plan the day's ride and possible side trips accordingly.

CLOTHING

Dressing for mountain riding is different from dressing for riding at lower elevations. Weather can, and does, change very rapidly in the mountains, and a day which starts out as a cloudless one can end up in a violent thunderstorm. For this reason, I always carry a heavy wool sweater since wool can help keep you warm even when wet. I also carry a water repellent jacket made of Goretex—a new fabric that breathes thus allowing perspiration to escape, but which doesn't allow raindrops to seep through. I also include wool mittens and a rain poncho. The latter I find helpful in a real downpour, since it helps to cover up my bare legs and adds an extra layer for warmth. If space permits, you might also bring arm and leg warmers and rain pants, also made of Goretex.

2

I feel strongly that bicyclists riding in the mountains should include helmets as a necessary item. Since the mountain roads are often very steep and full of curves, a helmet is your best protection against injury should you ever lose control.

PACKING

Panniers are constructed of waterproof material, but the zippers do tend to leak. If you pack your clothing in small plastic bags and place them in a larger garbage bag, you will never have to deal with arriving at your destination with wet clothing. I have emptied a lot of water out of the bottom of my panniers when riding in the rain, but at least this method protected my clothing.

WEATHER

Mountain riding invariably brings you face to face with rapidly changing weather conditions. When your day's ride involves crossing a pass or riding anywhere above timberline, you should be particularly aware of the day's forecast.

If the forecast calls for an approaching cold front, I generally find that the mornings still stay relatively clear for riding, but around noon, after the sun has had a chance to heat up the earth's surface, any moisture accompanying the front will begin producing clouds which will often lead to thunderheads by afternoon.

If there's a warm front in the area, you can expect drizzle and rain, and these rains tend to be longer lasting.

If the rain isn't part of a frontal system, but is caused by local build-ups that generally occur over the mountain during summer afternoons, you can often wait them out for one half to three quarters of an hour and then be treated to clearing skies.

I'm sure everyone is fully aware of the danger associated with lightning. If you're caught out in the open, abandon the metal lightning rod you're riding and seek shelter in a dense forest if there's one around. Try to avoid standing beneath a natural lightning rod such as a tall isolated tree or a telephone pole, or standing on any hilltop. If you're caught in an open area, seek shelter in a low place such as

3

a ravine or valley.

If you're above timberline, crouch down away from your bike so you don't become the target for the next lightning strike. If you feel your hair standing on end or hear the metallic items on your clothing begin to buzz, you know lightning is about to strike, so get down! Scientists at NOAA suggest that you drop to your knees and bend forward, putting your hands on your knees. They caution that you not lie flat on the ground.

One type of cloud that bicyclists should be aware of is the broad lens-shaped lenticular cloud. These are associated with high winds blowing from west to east and can be a particular problem when they reach speeds in excess of 40 miles per hour. These clouds form along the ridgetops of the mountains and can extend eastward for several hundred miles. Cycling above timberline on such days can be a true challenge!

You can become your own weather forecaster by watching the various clouds as they form overhead. If the clouds are high cirrus, forming above 20,000 feet, and resembling ice crystals, you can generally expect a nice day. As the clouds begin to form at lower levels, you can expect precipitation to occur. These lower clouds resemble patchy layers of puffy roll-like clouds or layers of clouds and are made of very small water droplets.

Cumulus clouds, puffy and cauliflower shaped, are often referred to as fair weather clouds unless they get enough lift from crossing the mountains to form thunderheads. When they become gray and towering, they can reach altitudes of up to 75,000 feet and rain, hail, and much electrical activity may be expected.

TEMPERATURES

One other factor to keep in mind in mountain riding is the rate at which the temperature drops as you climb higher: from 3 to 5 degrees per thousand feet. When wind accompanies this temperature drop, and it often does, you can become chilled very rapidly. This is when a windproof jacket and wool gloves can be a life saver.

Cumulonimbus forming over Harvard Peak—This one packed quite a whallop of rain and hail

Cumulus clouds ring the towering peaks

5

MOUNTAIN PASS COMMENTS

In checking the routes, the following areas warranted a great deal of vigilance on my part:

(1) *Rabbit Ears Pass from Kremmling to the summit.* This road doesn't have any shoulder for riding. The highway is heavily traveled by the 18-wheeler trucks. As a result, whenever two trucks approached from opposite directions, I got off onto the dirt shoulder and waited until they had passed. I found that very often the drivers would give me a small margin of room with their cabs, but would begin swinging their trailers back in too soon, often narrowly missing me.

The vacuum set up by these trucks traveling past at high speeds can be harrowing and very dangerous to the cyclist, so extreme caution should be exercised.

The west side of this pass didn't prove to be as great a problem since we were moving more with the flow of the traffic. If you ride up this pass from the west side, you will encounter a 7 percent grade for over 7 miles, but you will also have a climbing lane almost all the way.

(2) *Glenwood Canyon.* This is an exceptionally scenic

Top of Independence Pass—Bells in background

ride, but also very dangerous for a cyclist. Once you start down the canyon from Dotsero, the road narrows and has many blind curves making it impossible for you to be seen until the last minute. It is also heavily traveled by recreational vehicles which also leave very little room for you to ride.

If you do decide to risk it, exercise extreme caution. Both the Colorado State Highway Department and this writer assume no responsibility for your safety on this, or any other state highway.

(3) *Independence Pass*. The bottom of this pass begins with a nice riding shoulder, but as you climb higher, you will encounter three stretches of road where it becomes very narrow. As you ride along the right side of these narrows, you will often be looking down into a vast amount of open space, so be extremely careful while riding through here, particularly when being passed by the many recreational vehicles.

STARTING POINT

Since most of the rides begin in Boulder, the tourer has the opportunity of visiting one of several shops to purchase any last-minute equipment prior to beginning the tour. Some of the shops include: Bicycle Center, 2445 30th; Hartley Alley's Touring Cyclist Shop, 2639 Spruce; High Wheeler, 1015 Pearl, or The Spoke, 1301 Pennsylvania.

Since much of your time will be spent in areas where there are no bike shops for miles, I would advise the cyclist to be prepared to cope with many on-the-road repairs.

For this reason, I always carry a couple of extra tubes, an extra tire, tools for changing a tire, extra brake pads and cable, tube patching kit, medium screwdriver for adjusting gear positions or for digging your chain out of your freewheel. I also carry a package of wash and dry pads for cleaning up after a repair job.

While in Boulder, you might wish to take advantage of some of the scenic rides available prior to starting out in earnest on your mountain tour. In this way, you can build up your mountain legs and endurance by cycling up NCAR, Flagstaff, or up one of the nearby canyons. Detailed ride descriptions are available from my other cycling book entitled *Bike Rides of the Colorado Front Range*.

The Boulder area also has a multitude of possibilities for hiking. For trail descriptions, see my hiking book, *Hiking Trails of the Boulder Mountain Area.*

Many visitors to Boulder enjoy visiting the downtown mall where itinerant performers of music, mime, and magic may be seen. A stroll through the CU campus is always a stroll through beauty as well.

Motels in town include: Rodeway Inn (499-4422); Harvest House (443-3850); Boulder Travelodge (449-7550); and the Boulder Inn (499-3800).

Kinetic boat race—Boulder Reservoir

SOUTHERN COLORADO

Distance Traveled

Boulder—Golden 17
Golden—Idaho Springs 20
Idaho Springs—Dillon 39
Dillon—Vail 32
Vail—Glenwood 63
Glenwood—Parachute 45
Parachute—Delta 97
Delta—Montrose 21
Montrose—Ridgway 27
Ridgway—Telluride 68
Telluride—Dolores 96
Dolores—Mesa Verde 47
Mesa Verde—Durango 81
Durango—Silverton 49
Silverton—Ouray 23
Ouray—Montrose 37
Montrose—turnoff to Lake City 48
Montrose—Lake City 55
Lake City—Del Norte 84
Del Norte—Salida 81
Salida—Royal Gorge 50
Royal Gorge—Colorado Springs 59
Colorado Springs—Denver 70

1,209

Elevation Gain

Boulder—Loveland Pass 6592
Dillon over Vail Pass 923
Parachute—Grand Mesa 4900
Montrose—Telluride 2951
Cortez—Mesa Verde 2540
Durango—Molas Pass 3398
Pagosa Springs—Wolf Creek Pass 3771
Silverton—Red Mountain Pass 1700
Durango—Wolf Creek 3700
Gunnison—Monarch Pass 3609
Lake City—Slumgullion Pass 2660
Villa Grove—Poncha Pass 1030

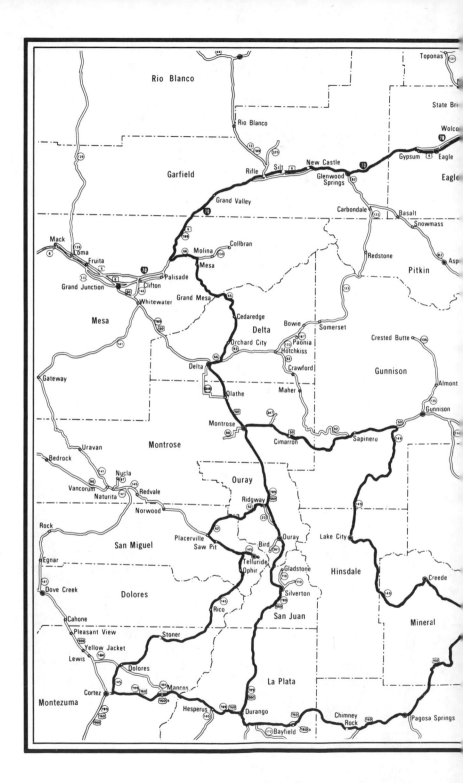

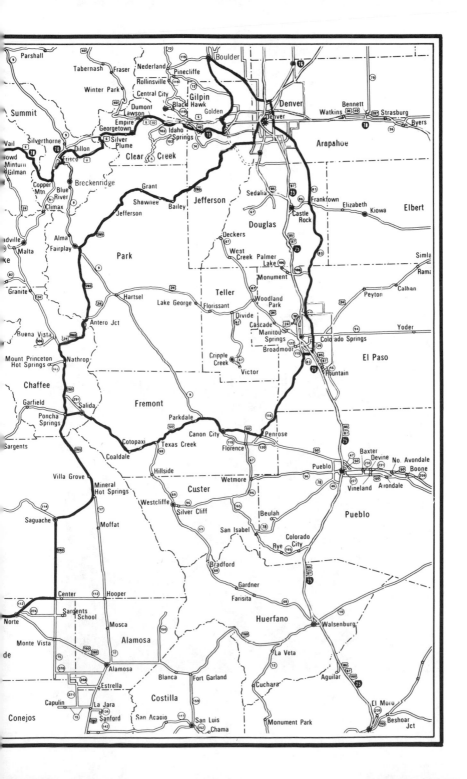

Glacially carved valley above Telluride

Southern Colorado: San Juans

Beginning in Boulder, cycle south on Highway 93 to Golden. Exercise extreme caution on this road since after you leave the intersection of Highways 93 and 128 at the top of the long hill, the road becomes very narrow with no shoulder for riding. This road generally becomes level until it crosses Highway 72 after which it drops down a long hill and becomes a roller coaster road the rest of the way into Golden. Very heavy truck traffic begins on this stretch of the road, necessitating defensive riding. As if to offset this dangerous stretch, you are finally treated to 1 mile of bike path as you near Golden.

Cycle south through Golden on Washington Avenue to 19th Avenue. Turn right and cycle up the hill 1 mile to Highway 6. Turn left at the light at 6th Avenue and 19th and ride southeast to the next traffic light. Turn right onto Highway 93 for a short stretch to meet Highway 6 again (below Heritage Square).

Turn right onto Highway 6 and continue 2 more miles to the next traffic light. Turn west to ride up the Mt. Vernon Canyon Road, Highway 40. Climb 6 miles to Exit 254 at Genessee Park. Ride along the right hand shoulder of I-70 for 2 miles, bypassing the exit to Chief Hosa, continuing on to Exit 242 to El Rancho. You will see signs along this route directing bicycles on and off the Interstate.

Turn right again to cross over the Interstate by El Rancho and pick up Highway 40 again. Continue westbound, coasting down Floyd Hill to the Interstate. Ride along the right shoulder of I-70 for 1.3 miles to Exit 243 at Hidden Valley.

Follow the frontage road from here to Idaho Springs. You will encounter a 1 mile section of dirt here, but then you'll have a paved road the rest of the way. East of town, cross over I-70 to ride into town.

Continue to Georgetown via the frontage road, crossing I-70 3 more times.

Now the climb begins in earnest. Leaving Georgetown via the right shoulder of I-70, cycle 5 miles to Silver Plume and Exit 226 to cycle along the frontage road 4.3 miles to Bakerville. Here you'll return to I-70 where you'll climb 5.1 more miles to the exit for Loveland Pass via Highway 6.

Climb Loveland Pass, whose summit is 11,992 feet, and coast down to Dillon.

From Dillon, cycle over the Dillon Reservoir along Dillon Dam Road and continue to Frisco. Once in town, cycle east towards town along Main Street a short distance, watching for bicycle sign #76 off to the south to pick up a separate

Dillon Reservoir as seen from Highway 6, Loveland Pass

bikepath that runs along Ten Mile Creek towards Copper Mountain for 7 miles with a 580 foot elevation gain. The bikepath terminates at the west end of the Copper Mountain complex. From here, you pick up the National Recreation Trail built for bikers and hikers which climbs Vail Pass, keeping mostly in the valley between the two lanes of the Interstate.

Once on top of the pass, you'll come to a newly constructed rest area where you can refill your water bottles before continuing down the west side. Exercise caution on this side since it is very steep in places, with a 14 percent grade, and has some sandy curves along the way. Vail Pass summit is 10,666 feet.

If you plan to camp along the pass, watch for the Gore Creek Campground off on the north side of the road about three quarters of the way down.

If you plan to stay overnight in Vail in a motel, you might try the Christiana at Vail (476-2261); Kiandra Lodge (476-4081); Lodge at Vail (476-5011); Ram's Horn Lodge (476-5646); Talisman Lodge (476-6522); and Valhalla at Vail (476-5641).

Cycle through Vail using the frontage road that parallels the Interstate. At Exit 173 at West Vail, you will ride along the right hand shoulder of I-70 for 2.5 miles to Minturn. At this point, you have the choice of either continuing to ride along the shoulder of I-70, or getting off the interstate and riding along Highway 6/24. This road was the primary route prior to the construction of I-70. It isn't heavily traveled, although it doesn't offer you the wide riding shoulder that the interstate does.

1 mile west of Minturn, you come to the Cliff Side Campground. 15 miles further, you reach Edwards, a truck stop with food available. At Eagle, you come to the Double Tree Best Western (328-6316) and Rueben's Restaurant. Gypsum offers both food and lodging. Camping is available. 1.5 miles west of Gypsum on Highway 6/24 along the Eagle River.

From Gypsum the Interstate hasn't been completed yet (December, 1981), so you will follow Highway 6/24 down through one of the most scenic gorges in the state: Glenwood Canyon. Here you ride down 18 miles below sheer rock walls banded with limestone, granite, and red sandstone which tower 1,000 feet above the Colorado River. Fortunately, you are going downhill, so you can enjoy it even more. There is heavy traffic through here, however, with many trucks and cars pulling travel trailers, creating a tight squeeze in many places. The road has no riding shoulder, so extreme caution should be exercised!

Many kayaks and rubber rafts may be seen shooting their way among the rapids of the river. To try one of these rides, watch for the outfitters located along the canyon.

For a 1 mile hike up to an incredible spot, Hanging Lake, watch for the turn off to the north midway down the canyon. The trail is steep (1000 feet), but seeing the lake and its many vine-covered slopes is well worth the time and effort.

Once in Glenwood you have a wide selection of places to stay and eat, which are described in the Central Colorado tour (see page 72). You may also camp in one of the campgrounds in town.

From Glenwood, you will need to ride along the right shoulder of the Interstate to Exit 114 where you again have the option of either getting off the Interstate and following Highway 6/24 where you'll encounter less traffic, or continuing along the shoulder of the Interstate.

There is food and lodging at New Castle, 11 miles out of Glenwood, as well as a campground with its own laundromat.

Continue 8.4 miles to Silt where you will find a grocery store and a place to eat.

Rifle, at 5354 feet, and 7 miles farther, serves at the gateway to Dinosaur National Monument. Here you'll find a 7-Eleven Store for picking up lunch supplies, or Mc's Cafe, Audrey's Cafe, the Cozy Corner Cafe, and the Shale Motel.

The route from Glenwood to Rifle becomes much drier with lots of sagebrush and sunshine.

As you proceed towards Grand Junction, you can see the Book Cliff Mountains, site of large quantities of oil shale. Geologists estimate that at least a thousand billion barrels of high quality petroleum is locked in these rocks which was recently the site of some oil shale mining.

From Rifle it is 16 miles to Parachute where there is a great deal of freshly picked fruit to be sampled along with camping facilities.

15 miles out of Parachute, you pass another campground beside the river.

Pool at Glenwood Springs

30 miles from Parachute, take the turn-off at Exit 49 for Grand Mesa, an immense basalt tableland, onto Highway 65. There is no shoulder along this road which climbs below some massive sandstone walls along Plateau Creek. It is a good, steady climb from this intersection up to Mesa, but it's short.

In Mesa, you can purchase goodies from the general store or eat at the Toothpick Cafe. Eugene's Cafe, across the street, is only open Thursday-Sunday from 6-9 in the evening and is more expensive.

Continue on to Powderhorn Ski Area's turn-off where you can stay at the Chalet Lodge (268-5410).

1 mile further you cross a cattle guard, so be careful.

4.6 miles further, you come to the Mesa Lakes Recreation Area. You will be climbing steadily all the way to here, and by the time you reach the top of the mesa, you will be at 10,600 feet where you can enjoy the cool, quiet of the largest flat-top mountain in the world. Over 200 lakes cover its top, and on a clear day you can see for over 200 miles. The valley floor is 5700 feet below you, and the wild flowers in these meadows are extremely beautiful.

At the Mesa Lakes Recreation Area you can find food

and lodging at the Mesa Lakes Resort (268-5467) or camp in the Jumbo Campground nearby. Now's your chance to do some great fishing and boating.

Should you decide to do some hiking, cross the reservoir in front of the lodge and pick up the road leading to the summer cabins. Follow this road to its cul-de-sac and continue beyond to pick up the West End Trail which terminates 10 miles later at Palisade Point.

For a shorter hike to another of the glacially carved lakes in the area, follow the same road, bypassing the summer cabin turn off, and continue to the next lake where there are picnic tables and additional fishing. There you'll find a trail to Lost Lake 1 mile away via the Mesa Lake Trail.

Continuing on .6 mile from Mesa Lakes, you come to Spruce Grove Campground. Little Bear and Island Lake Campgrounds are 8 miles further away, along with the Grand Beach Cabins and Trail Lake View Cabins.

1 mile further you come to 4 more campgrounds: Valley View, Carp Lake, Ward Lake located 1 mile east, and Kiser Creek, 2 miles further to the east.

You will also pass Mesa Lakes Resort (268-5467) and Grand Mesa Lodge (856-3211) which offer hiking from the lodge. 1 paved trail from here goes to Lake View Point where you can see Island Lake plus 10 to 12 others. Hiking to the east, you come to Craig Crest Trail where you hike up an easy grade to the top and along the edge of the mesa. From Lands' End Road, you can look down into the valley, 1 mile deep and 30 miles wide.

As you come off the top of the mesa, you will eventually pass the Southgate Inn and Motel (874-9726). There is a good riding shoulder along this highway all the way into Cedaredge at 6100 feet. Here you can get a bite at the Squat and Gobble Bakery, or stay at the Tri Motor Motel (856-3222); the Cedaredge Lodge (856-3727); or the Alexander Lake Lodge (856-3218).

5 miles out of Cedaredge you pass a grocery store with good, freshly picked apples available from the local orchards.

4 miles further, you pass through Cory with another grocery store.

At the intersection of Highways 65 and 92, you pick up a divided highway with a nice, wide shoulder for riding.

2 miles from this intersection, you come to the KOA

18

Campground (874-3918) complete with a pool and located next to a Kentucky Fried Chicken place. Mine Shack Restaurant is 1 mile further down the road close to Sonic Happy Eating.

The cities at the foot of the Grand Mesa including Austin, Cory, Eckert, Orchard City, and Cedaredge are all full of many orchards producing peaches, pears, apricots and cherries. 75 percent of Colorado's apples are grown in this valley.

During the second week in July, you can attend the Surface Creek Festival featuring dancing, a town barbecue, parade, art show, and the Little Britches Rodeo, all held in Cedaredge.

At one time, Delta was inhabited by the Ute Indians. Later the area became important in the early Spanish exploration of the Southwest. Originally it was called Uncompahgre after the Uncompahgre River, but was changed to Delta when the pronunciation proved to be so difficult. Because of its elevation of 4980 feet, Delta has a very mild, dry climate with an average summer temperature of 68 to 75 degrees and a growing season of 146 days.

Cleland Park in town has a nice picnic area, tennis courts, campground and a year-round swimming pool.

Places to stay include: El D Rado Motel (874-4493); Sundance Motel (874-9781); and the Southgate Inn (874-9726).

There are two bike shops here: Delta Bicycle at 2nd and Main, and Delta Hardware Company at 3rd and Main.

Sweitzer Lake, 3 miles south of Delta, is a great fishing site.

A Delta KOA is located 1 mile east of town on Highway 92.

From Delta, you continue along Highway 50, and 11 miles later you pass Olathe where there is another campground.

Montrose is 21 miles from Delta, and being a good-sized town offers several places for staying overnight: Best Western Red Arrow Motel (249-9641), Black Canyon Motel (249-3495), Chief Motel (249-4595), Lazy IG Motel (249-4567), San Juan Inn (249-6644), Trapper Motel (249-3426), and Western Motel (249-3481). Montrose is 5794 feet.

During the 1880's this city was the railroad distribution point for passengers and freight which was headed into the San Juan mining towns. Today it is the center of 3 national forests with abundant fishing.

The natural beauty of the area is reflected in its name

given by the town's founder, who was reminded of the beautiful country of Scotland described in Sir Walter Scott's *Legend of Montrose.*

For fans of early Colorado history, be sure to visit the Ute Indian Museum 4 miles south of town on US 550. This memorial to the Ute Indians honoring Chief Ouray and his wife, Chipeta, gives a good description of the Utes when they lived in the area. It's open from July through Labor Day from 9:30 to 5:30 daily. A fee is charged for admission.

12 miles south of Montrose on Highway 550, you pass a cafe.

14 miles further is the Sunset Motel and Cafe at Ridgway.

Ridgway, whose elevation has climbed up to 6983 feet, is in the center of an open valley surrounded by many majestic peaks such as Mt. Sneffels, Court House, Chimney Peak, and the entire Dallas Range. The area was the setting for several movies including "How the West Was Won," and "True Grit."

High temperatures in this area only reach into the 80's.

After 1 mile, you turn onto Highway 82 to ride to Telluride. This road crosses Dallas Divide at 8870 feet before dropping down into Placerville where there is a grocery store.

Turn onto Highway 145 to cycle to the ski town of Telluride. The grade into Telluride is a steep one, climbing to 8745 feet. Along the way, 2 miles out of Placerville, are the Blue Jay Cabins and Cafe; 1 mile further: Fall Creek Campground; and 1 more mile: Sawpit with a deli and store. After 5 miles, you pass an unmarked campground located along a stream. From the intersection at Highway 145, it is 16 miles to Telluride.

Telluride, referred to as the "Valley of the Hot Springs," is located at the head of a beautiful glacial valley from which many rivers descend to continue down the red rock canyon you cycled through to arrive here. The name of the town comes from a type of silver and gold ore, found in the presence of tellurium, called telluride ore. The town once had a population of nearly 5,000 people, 30 bars, and numerous other gaming houses and bordellos. The New Sheridan Hotel is the place where William Jennings Bryan gave his "Cross of Gold" speech in 1902. The opera house was built in 1891 and still retains the original main roll cur-

Along Cascade Fall Trail

tain and complete stage settings of the time.

Telluride has been designated as a national historic landmark. It had the first long distance alternating current system in the world which was used to light the town and power the surrounding mines.

The city was founded in 1875 and contains 350 miles of tunnels which have been drilled into the mountains around town, enough to reach from San Francisco to Los Angeles. Billions of dollars of gold, silver, copper, lead, and zinc have been mined here since 1880, and the area is still being mined. The early gold miners called the city "To Hell you ride."

Today the town is famous for its skiing (with an average 400 inches of snowfall) and the fact that Butch Cassidy robbed his first bank here.

Attractions in the town include the Annual Bluegrass and Country Music Festival which traditionally takes place at the foot of the awesome San Juan Mountains the last part of June. Here you can see the works of many artists and craftspeople from all over the country. If you're a picker, you're invited to bring your instrument along to do some of your own picking "out among the trees." For information, contact the Telluride Bluegrass and Country Music Festival, Telluride, Colorado 81435, or call 728-3437.

The Galloping Goose Bicycle Tour is also held in June—a one week family-oriented tour of the San Juan Mountains tracing the historic Galloping Goose train route. The Galloping Goose was one of the last narrow gauge passenger trains that was pulled by an automobile engine. It was used to transport freight and passengers to Telluride. For information on this tour, write to the Chamber of Commerce, Box 653, Telluride, Colorado 81435, or call 728-3614.

On July 4th, the town begins its activities at dawn, and continues until midnight, including a great fireworks display.

A hang glider invitational is held in mid-August. Pilots from all over the world come to step off the 12,000 foot peak. Also the Chamber Music Festival holds concerts at the historical Sheridan Opera House. A film festival is held in town in early September.

Along Telluride's main street

There is great hiking in Telluride as well. For a 2 mile hike, go up to the Wasach Trail through Bear Creek Canyon to see seven waterfalls. It's reached by going south from town up Pine Street.

For another hike, climb up to the Liberty Bell Mine, a steep 3 mile hike up to one of the largest mines, to see more mining ruins. Take Tomboy Road north out of town. This trail/four wheel drive road crosses over Imogene Pass into Ouray.

You can either hike or ride east out of town to see Bridal Veil and Ingram Falls. Located 1 mile east, these falls are Colorado's highest vertical falls. At the top of the falls is one of the many early hydroelectric plants which have provided power to the mills at the various mines.

There is good fishing in over 100 mountain lakes in the area which are well stocked with trout.

Places to stay include the Sheridan Hotel (728-4351); Bushwacker Inn (728 3303); Manitou Inn (728-4311); Victorian Inn (728-3684); Dahl Haus (728-9915); Telluride Lodge (728-3831); and Tomboy Inn (728-3871).

Places to eat include: Powder House Restaurant, Sofia's Restaurant, Floradora Restaurant, Iron Ladle or Thunderchicken.

Telluride Sports has a bicycle shop.

As you cycle out of Telluride via Highway 145 and turn south, you pass Sunshine Campground. 5 miles later, you

Wilson Peak on Lizard Head Pass

23

pass Matterhorn Campground, and 2 miles later the Trout Lake Campground, the latter probably one of the most scenic of all the campgrounds in the area. The climb through here is mostly uphill and is a strenuous ride.

Lizard Head Pass' summit is 10,250 feet. At the top you can see a lush alpine meadow with sun-sparkling lakes, towering thirteeners and fourteeners dwarfing you as you ride by. Drop down into the forest now with more water and rivers. This will be a flower-carpeted ride with yellow and purple flowers blooming everywhere.

2 miles past the summit, you come to a trail leading past Lizard Head which is visible from the highway. This trail joins the Lizard Head Trail which is the route up Wilson Peak. There are 2 other fourteeners here too: El Diente and Mt. Wilson, the former considered to be a very difficult climb because of its knife ridge.

7 miles below Trout Lake Campground you reach Priest Gulch and Caylor Campgrounds.

Continue to drop down to Rico at 8827 feet where you can purchase lunch at the Galloping Goose Restaurant or stay at the Rico Motel (967-2444). The town, though small, has a park in its center for picnicking.

19 miles below Rico you'll pass another campground. 30 miles below this campsite is the Stoner Creek Campground and Lodge.

32 miles below Stoner Creek is West Dolores Road and more camping.

39 miles further: Trouthaven Campground.

The ride through here is on a road that didn't have much traffic when we rode it, and dropped steadily to Dolores at 6936 feet. The landscape gets steadily drier and the temperatures warmer.

In Dolores you can see another Galloping Goose train like the one you saw in Telluride. This town was also the site of the Dominguez-Escalante Expedition on July 29, 1776. Their goal was to open a route from Santa Fe to the California Spanish missions to begin the conversion of the Indians to Spanish culture and religion. The Franciscans' journal and maps were the first record of the land and people of Colorado and Utah.

Motels in Dolores include the El Benado Motel (882-7203) and the Rio Grande Southern Hotel (882-9988).

From Dolores, you ride 8 more miles to the intersection with Highway 289 outside of Cortez. Places to stay here include the Aneth Lodge (565-3453); Arrow Motel (565-3755); Bel Rau Lodge (565-3638); Best Western Sands (565-3761); El Capri Motel (565-3764); and the Lazy Ge Motel (565-8577).

Restaurant possibilities include the Bell Creek Rig and Refinery located three quarters of a mile east of town on US 160, and the Pony Express in the city.

If you want to stay on the outskirts of town, try the Larry G Campground and Motel. Gold Thieves Restaurant is right across the street. There is also a KOA Campground here.

Highway 160 towards Mesa Verde has a very good riding shoulder. It's 8 miles to the turnoff to Mesa Verde.

The climb up to Mesa Verde is a good one, climbing over 21 miles from 6936 feet at Dolores to 8572 feet. Caution: This road is narrow in places and passes through one short tunnel.

Camping in the park may be done at the Morfield Campground Village complex with almost 500 individual and group campsites available. You cannot reserve spaces, so an early arrival is advised. Campsites cannot be left unattended for more than 24 hours.

Cliff Palace

To stay in a motel right in the area, for which reservations are a must during the summer tourist season, call ahead to the Far View Motor Lodge (529-4421).

Mesa Verde offers 1,000 year old ruins, mysteriously abandoned by the "Anasazi" 700 years ago. Some of the dwellings which were built on top of the high mesa gave the "Ancient Ones" a view of 6 major mountain ranges and over 30,000 square miles of alpine and desert scenery.

Asphalt roads lead to the principal ruins. The Wetherill Mesa, however, may only be toured by bus which starts adjacent to the Far View Visitor Center parking lot. It's a 12 mile ride.

However, you can tour by bicycle along the Chapin Mesa. The road drops down to 6969 feet from Far View's 8040 feet. You are able to tour most of the ruins located along the 2 ten kilometer roads. If you plan to visit Balcony House, which was the only guided tour offered (in 1980), plan to get there as early as possible or you could be in for a long wait. The other ruins are open to the public without a guide and pamphlets or signs explain the history of the area.

Spruce Tree House was an interesting place. Living quarters were only 6 by 8 by 5.5 feet. Obviously, when the weather was good, everyone lived outdoors.

It was also interesting to note that the Indians discarded most of their refuse in trash mounds heaped both in front and in back of their living quarters. Here they also buried some of their dead, presumably because this was one of the easiest places to dig during the winter.

Picnic sites with restrooms are located along each of the Ruin Road loops.

Mesa Verde can be very hot during the summer, with highs ranging from 85 to 100 degrees. However, evenings cool off considerably ranging from 55 to 65 degrees. Morfield Campground is at 7800 feet, and Far View Lodge at 8080 feet, so you certainly won't need air conditioning to sleep cool.

After you have been steeped in the archeology and history of Mesa Verde, coast back down to the highway and ride east towards Durango on Highway 160. Watch for Shiprock in front of you as you descend from Mesa Verde. It's a very striking rock formation which resembles a ship in full sail towering 1400 feet above the plains.

.5 mile east of the turnoff from Mesa Verde you pass the Lazy G Campground. 9 miles later in Mancos you can also camp at the United Campground.

Mancos also has accommodations: Mesa Verde Motel (533-7741); Silver Peaks Motel; and Enchanted Mesa (553-7729).

6 miles from Mancos is another campground: Thompson Peak.

9 miles later: Canyon Motel and Cafe.

10 miles: Cherry Creek Campground.

13 miles: Kroeger Campground.

From Hesperus, the highway becomes much wider with two lanes climbing to the east. After passing Mancos you begin the climb. We encountered road construction (in 1980) along a short stretch here, but otherwise it's a great riding road.

Arriving in Durango at 6512 feet, we entered what was once one of the wildest cities in the west, with Billy the Kid being a frequent visitor. The infamous Stockton-Eskridge gang once engaged local lawmen in a gunbattle that lasted for over an hour along the town's main street. It boomed as a mining town in the 1800's when it served as a railroad hub for the agricultural and mining area of the San Juans.

The first weekend in August features the Navajo Trails Fiesta with 2 rodeo performances, Indian dances, parades, and horse racing.

While in town, you might try to visit the Durango Fish Hatchery, one of the largest trout hatcheries with a capacity of 10 million fry.

From here you can ride one of the last regularly scheduled narrow gauge trains in the United States. The train departs each morning from Durango for the 45 mile trip to Silverton pulling you through the heart of the Southern Rockies. Reservations are required and should be made at least one month prior to your departure by calling either the Rio Grande ticket office (247-2733), or through Denver (629-5533). You may purchase one way tickets which are good for passage only on the date of sale if one way space is available. You can arrange to return to Durango by bus.

The train ride both ways takes all day, and each year over 100,000 people ride this route which was first laid in 1882

Train—Silverton

in a record 9 months and 5 days. The round trip fare in 1980 was $16 for adults.

The train has a 2 hour layover in Silverton to allow you time to look around town.

Places to stay in Durango include: Alpine North Motel (247-4042); Best Western Durango Inn (247-3251); Silver Spur (247-5552); Ramada Inn (259-1010); and Edelweiss Motel (247-5685).

Places to eat include Assay Office Restaurant, The Cellar, The Palace Restaurant, and the Silver Spur Restaurant.

Camping is available north of town at United Campground, Lazy U Campground, Herman Meadows Campground, or the KOA.

10 miles further north you come to Needles Country Store. It's a good climb to here, and then the road becomes hilly.

From Durango, you need to make a choice of either turning north to ride to Silverton and Ouray via the Million Dollar Highway or continue east along Highway 160 for 60 miles to Pagosa Springs. Because of the road construction along Wolf Creek Pass, we rode to Silverton, but the alternate route will be described later.

Riding towards Silverton, you pass the Purgatory Campground and ski area which also has a lodge. The ski area has a summer slide, like so many of the ski areas in the state.

5 miles beyond the ski area: Sig Creek Campground.

Now the road drops down for 1 mile beyond the ski area and then climbs up again for 7 miles to Coal Bank Hill, swinging east of Engineer Mountain. Coal Bank Hill is 10,600 feet.

2 miles further you pass the Lake Creek Burn area with a turnoff. A forest fire destroyed the area in 1875, and you can see a good example of the plant succession that follows a major fire.

After enjoying a flatter ride for 5 miles, you begin to climb up Molas Pass for 4 miles. 2.5 miles up, you come to the Lime Creek rest area, and 1.3 miles further to Andrews Lake which is only .4 of a mile below the summit at 10,910 feet. You can either enjoy a picnic lunch here or cross over the pass to Little Molas Lake if you prefer to get your climbing out of the way before you indulge.

.3 mile north of the summit you come to the Molas Lake Campground—a real beauty for camping.

A coast of 5.7 miles down a steep, winding grade brings you to Silverton at 9318 feet.

The town named for the well known quote, "There's silver by the ton in those mountains," is also known as the "mining community that never quits." Over 500 million dollars in metals have been mined here over the past 95 years. The town still boasts the original hitching posts, kerosene lamps, and the old sheriff's office.

Silverton had a remarkable saloon in its heyday plus a red light district on "notorious" Blair Street. At that time, they even hired Bat Masterson to patrol it. Many of the buildings along Main Street are the originals. Blair Street has been the location of numerous western movies, and the entire town is a registered National Historic District.

For a break from cycling, you might pick up a walking tour pamphlet and enjoy a stroll through town.

Imagine: a growing season of 14 days! Does that tell you something about the weather and altitude? Daytime summer temperatures range from 50 to 75 degrees, but nighttime temperatures drop down to 30 or 50 degrees. Mid-day showers are frequent here because of the hot air rising

Steep mountains ring Silverton

from the desert areas to the west.

There is a picnic table and public restroom available in town along Blair Street near the Chamber of Commerce.

Places to stay include: Grand Imperial Hotel (387-5527); Red Mountain Lodges and Motel (387-5512); Teller House Pension (387-5423); and the Triangle Motel (387-5780).

Camping is available in Hermosa Meadows located 9 miles north on US 550 and SR 789, and in Pinon Acres KOA 8 miles east on US 160. Red Mt. Lodges, a camper-trailer park, is in town.

Places to eat include: Miner's Pick Buffet located one block east of Main Street; Lemon Tree Restaurant; Gold King Diningroom; Zhivago's Restaurant; and the Teller House which boasts a fast take-out window for streakers.

Be sure to see the old jail built in 1893 which has now been converted to a curio shop. You can also tour the Silver Queen Mine and Museum.

Hardrockers' Holidays are held each year in mid-August in which individuals and teams compete in a tug-o-war, hand mucking, machine mucking and drilling.

The Kendall Mountain Footrace is held in July. For information contatct the Chamber of Commerce, P.O. Box 565, Silverton, 81433 (387-5654).

A beautiful local hike is to the Christ of the Mines Shrine on Anvil Mountain. A map is located at the information caboose on Blair Street.

Now for an unforgettable ride over the Million Dollar Highway, laid out by Otto Mears. Originally it was a toll road blasted out of sheer rock walls in 1881-83, with a grade that was too steep for the railroad. Tolls were charged then: $5 for a team and wagon and $1 for a horse and rider.

It's 10 miles to the top of Red Mountain. You'll climb many steep switchbacks for 6 miles from Silverton. The 3 Red Mountains visible to the east are among the state's more colorful peaks.

Leaving Silverton on Million Dollar Highway

31

Mines located along the north side produced over 12 million dollars in ore. Around the big bend in the road you can see an old mill on the left along with one of the last buildings left behind in Red Mountain Town when it burned down in 1892.

2 miles after completing the switchbacks off the top, you really get the effect of the sheer walls carved out of the sides of the mountain. Now you drop down into Ouray at 7014 feet and pass the Amphitheater Campground 2 miles southeast of town and 2 more miles east along a park road. Roaring Falls of Box Canyon is here too, where you can see some very steep vertical rock walls with a 285 foot waterfall. Admission is charged.

Motels in Ouray include: Alpine Motel (325-4546), Antlers Motel (325-4589), Box Canyon Motel (325-4551), Circle M Motel (325-4394), Ouray Chalet Motel (325-4331), and the Twin Peaks Motel (325-4427).

Ouray, named for the well known Ute Indian chief, was a favorite camping spot for the Indians who bathed in the hot springs bubbling from the valley floor. The town itself was originally established as a supply center for the rich mines in the area such as the Camp Bird Mine which gave its owner Thomas Walsh the wealth necessary to buy the Hope Diamond for his daughter.

The town that grew up here during the mining years was ultra modern. It had such niceties as electric lights, steam heat, hot and cold running water, and even marble-topped lavatories. The local boarding house offered an unheard of luxury for towns: free meals. All other mine boarding-houses charged from 25 to 35 cents a meal.

Sights to see here include the Cascade Falls reached by walking east .5 mile up 6th Avenue, a dirt street which narrows into a footpath.

For a great overlook of town from the Twin Falls Trail, follow 7th Avenue west past the 4 J Campground and cross the bridge. Turn left to go uphill and when at the top of the hill, turn right. The trail is steep, but quite scenic.

There are other trails available and a full description may be found by picking up a trail guide at the Chamber of Commerce located next to the mineral pool north of town. Descriptions are also included in the town's free newspaper: *Ouray-Ridgway: Switzerland of America Vacation*

Guide, available in most motels.

For a fantastic wild flower display, see if you can catch a ride up to Yankee Boy Basin, a gravel road not suitable for riding. The area is also the trailhead for Mt. Sneffels. This mountain involves a couloir ascent which is often filled with snow year-round. The basin below it will stagger your imagination with its riot of color.

Be sure to take a refreshing dip in the mineral pool north of town. It's 250 by 150 feet with a large center area for long distance swimmers who enjoy swimming laps. It's fed by spring water which heats the water to 156 degrees. After the city adds some cold water, pool temperatures range from 85 to 95 degrees. The pool is closed on Mondays when it's drained and refilled. Be sure to end your swim before sundown, which comes early in this valley ringed by steep rock walls. The air get very cold after sundown, making your trip from the warm pool to the bathhouse a very chilling experience.

Ouray: ringed by steep red rocks walls

If you wish to visit a health spa, try the Weisbaden Spa and Health Resort 2 blocks east of Main Street. They offer a full health spa program complete with sauna, vapor cave, and swimming pool.

The first week in August features an Artists' Alpine Holiday, a gathering place for artists from all over the state.

Anyone a cyclist-marathoner? How about this one: running from Ouray to Telluride? Contact the Chamber of Commerce in Ouray for details.

After you decide to tear yourself away from the fantastic beauty of this area, continue north on Highway 50. The road is generally level and it is 25 miles to Montrose.

If, in Durango, you decide to continue east into Pagosa Springs, you will have rolling terrain all the way into town. From Pagosa Springs, you climb over Wolf Creek Pass, covering 42 miles to reach South Fork. The climb is steep, climbing up to 10,850 feet from 7079 feet at Pagosa Springs.

There are some nice campgrounds along the route from Pagosa Springs: Elk Meadows 5 miles east on US 160; Wolf Creek Campground 16 miles from town; and West Fork Campground, 1 mile further west.

From Montrose, you have a different kind of scenery and beauty on your ride through the Curecanti National Recreation Area. The road along Highway 50 is a good one, and after 20 miles you begin to get some great views of this man-made reservoir complete with its many camping areas, boating, and fishing possibilities.

For an overview of the area, stop at the Blue Mesa Headquarters. Here you can also schedule a boat tour of the lake, best done 2 or 3 days in advance. The trip is 18 miles, and all seats are reserved. To make advance reservations, call 641-0403.

Blue Mesa Dam, formed by a 342 foot dam across the Gunnison River, is one of three lakes. It's the largest lake in the state, extending for 70 miles. All around its shoreline you can see signs of old volcanic activity complete with ash flows and lava beds. The area is also famous for its dinosaur bones.

Upon arriving at the eastern edge of the Blue Mesa, you have another choice to make. You can either continue eastbound along Highway 50 to Gunnison where you can stay at the Crescent Motel (641-1263); Dos Rios Motor Hotel

(641-1000); Harmel's Ranch Resort (641-1740); Tomichi Village Inn (641-1131); or the Western Motel (641-1722).

From Gunnison, you'll continue east on Highway 50 to cross over Monarch Pass to Salida as described in the Northern Rockies ride.

If you haven't had your fill of the San Juan's, turn south at the end of Blue Mesa to cycle to Lake City. Note: If you're considering taking a loop ride through Creede to South Fork, there's a 9 mile stretch of dirt road outside of Creede. It's rideable, but dusty, so you may wish to ride to Lake City and return to the Blue Mesa area.

If you decide to cycle to Lake City, reservations in this small town are recommended. Try the Western Belle (944-2241); G & M Cabins (944-2282); Silver Spur Motel

Downtown Lake City

(944-2231); Town Square Cabins (944-2236); Westwood Cabins (944-2205); Pleasant View Resort (944-2262); or the Matterhorn Motel (944-2210).

From the turn off at Blue Mesa you'll enjoy 4 miles of level riding before you begin climbing 10 miles. Be sure to watch for some unmarked cattle guards along this route.

While in town, ask about the trail leading to Cannibal Plateau where the graves of the 5 prospectors eaten by Alferd Packer in December, 1873, are located.

Leaving Lake City, you climb over Slumgullion Pass which tops out at 11,331 feet from 8671 feet at Lake City. Be sure to stop at the wide turn-out on the way up and get a good look at the San Cristobal Lake sparkling at your feet.

After Slumgullion Pass, you drop down slightly before climbing up a smaller pass, Spring Creek Pass, whose elevation is 10,901 feet and a climb of 2 more miles.

7.5 miles after the summit of Spring Creek Pass, be sure to watch for the turn-off to the left for North Clear Creek Falls. You will need to ride .8 mile along a dirt road to reach this very pretty waterfall which comes unexpectedly out of nowhere. Camping is also available here.

4 miles after the falls you come to a KOA Campground.

Be sure to watch for cattle guards along this road. 2.2 miles after you pass Santa Maria Lake, you begin the dirt stretch. The road is slightly downhill at first, but then it levels out. The dirt is hard packed, and, though slow, is rideable.

6 miles later you pass a campground.

8 miles further along, you reach Creede whose elevation is 8852 feet. Creede is another old mining town that has had mining activities conducted since the 1800's. At one time over 10,000 souls lived here, but now it boasts only 800 year-round residents. In the past, it was visited by such notorious people as Calamity Jane, Poker Alice, and is the site of the grave of Bob Ford, Jesse James's killer.

If time permits, visit the Creede Museum which displays an old hearse, old popcorn vendor, rock specimens, and other memorabilia from old mining days. It's open from 9 to 5 throughout the summer.

This whole area has great fishing. In the Creede area alone there are over 500 miles of fishable streams along with 52 lakes.

Places to stay in Creede include: Cotton Wood Cove and Restaurant (658-2242); Trailin' Inn Campground, 1 mile south of town; Big River Guest Ranch (658-2259); Blue Creek Lodge (658-2479); Snow Shoe Motel (658-2315); and Old Creede Hotel and Restaurant (658-2680).

For your picnic lunch, stop at the Creede Grocery in town. For a restaurant, try the Miner's Inn or La Casita.

Leaving Creede, you pass through much drier land with much cottonwood and sagebrush. Just outside of town you pass Wagon Wheel Gap which was used as the first toll gate on the old stagecoach road from Silverton to Lake City in 1874.

7 miles southwest of town, you pass Marshall Peak Campground.

Highway 149 then terminates in South Fork. Places to stay here include the Inn Motel (873-5514); Chinook Motel and Store; Rainbow Lodge and Grocery (873-5571); Pack A Way Inn (873-5581); Spruce Ski Lodge (873-9980); and Foothills Lodge (873-5969). Campgrounds include South Fork Campground, 3 miles southwest of town; Highway Spring, 4.5 miles southwest of town; Park Creek, 8 miles southwest of town; Ticker Ponds, 12 miles southwest of town and 3 miles south on US 160; and Big Meadows, 12 miles southwest of town.

From here you might wish to make a side trip up Wolf Creek Pass for some high altitude camping, or to enjoy the beauty of the area. Watch for the Continental Divide Overlook located on top of the pass. This road follows 2 miles of switchbacks along a good road from which you get a good overlook of the valley and mountains.

For those who still have the energy left for a hike, walk to Treasure Mountain Falls located on the west side of the pass. Watch for a switchback path that leads half way up a 105 foot vertical waterfall. There are treasure signs all along the path. Once there, you get close enough to the falls to actually feel the spray. A path across the bridge makes a loop hike back.

From South Fork it is 31 miles to Del Norte, a fairly flat, fast ride along the Rio Grande River, the third longest river in the US. You'll drop down from 8180 feet to 7874 feet.

Places to stay in Del Norte include: the Old West Hotel; Del Norte Motel, El Rancho Motel (657-3332); Rio Grande

Motel (657-2289); and the Pine Tree Motel located 14 miles out of town at the intersection with Highway 285.

Del Norte is one of Colorado's oldest towns. In the middle and latter part of the 19th century, it was a rendezvous point for the trappers, traders, and Indians. Today the town is involved in food and livestock shipping and processing.

Watch for the old mineral well right in the center of town.

Upon leaving Del Norte, you might wish to consider taking a side trip to the Sand Dunes National Monument. If so, this will add an extra day to your tour since the ride is approximately 50 miles from Center.

The sand dunes are located at the eastern edge of the great San Luis Valley of south central Colorado, and are the highest inland sand dunes in the US. They parallel the base of the 14,000 foot Sangre de Cristo Mountains for 10 miles and occupy 57 square miles. The sands are continually shifting, forming hills, ripples and beautiful wave patterns; however, this area can be very hot during the summer.

You can stay in the Pinyon Flats Campground right in the monument.

If you choose not to visit the dunes, continue along Highway 160 to Center and turn north to ride to Saguache. The Utes called Saguache 'Sa gua gua chi pa', meaning blue earth or water at the blue earth. The early trappers and fur traders couldn't pronounce the Indian name so they shortened it to its present name. The settlement was founded here in 1876.

The road from Saguache to Monte Vista was originally laid out by drawing a straight line for the route, alleged to be the longest stretch of absolutely straight road in the world.

Saguache provided jail facilities for the infamous Alferd Packer, condemned to die for cannibalism. In 1874, he was accused of eating portions of his 5 prospecting companions, but he managed to escape from the jail to remain free for 9 years.

Also you can visit the Saguache County Museum where you may view 7 different rooms depicting an old school room, mineral room and jail used to confine Packer, however briefly.

A motel here is the N Lazy R Motel (655-2233).

Now you ride 19 miles to Villa Grove, which was established in the 1870's not as a mining town, but as a supply point for the valley ranchers and mining camps. During the 1800's, it was completely surrounded by trees. The town also served as a terminal for the narrow gauge railroad from Poncha Pass. It has an eating spot available: Katie's Kitchen.

From here, you begin your ride up Poncha Pass, which is not a difficult climb, from 7980 feet at Villa Grove to the summit at 9010 feet. On the way you pass the Gingerbread Ranch Campground 1 mile north of the summit.

The ride becomes less dry and more lush as you enter the forested land near the summit.

Now coast down into Poncha Springs at 7469 feet where you pass the old Jackson Lodge and Hotel built in 1878. It once served as a stopping place for travelers to Gunnison and Leadville. People often came here to seek relief from their aches and pains in the nearby hot springs. The rooms in the hotel have been named after well known people such as the James brothers: Jesse and Frank, H.A.W. Tabor, Susan B. Anthony, and others. For reservations, call 539-3122.

You can also stay at the Rocky Mountain Lodge in Poncha Springs (539-6008).

From Poncha Springs, if your time is short, you will probably continue north on Highway 285 to Buena Vista to continue back to Denver.

However, it you have the time to visit the Royal Gorge, returning to Denver via Colorado Springs, continue on to Salida which offers many accommodations including the Best Western (539-2514); Western Holiday (539-2553); Hi Lander Motel (539-4134); Motel Martha (539-4722); Redwood Lodge (539-2528); and West Wind Motel (539-6695).

Salida means "outlet", which is what the town was originally set up for—outfitting the numerous mining camps. It was originally intended to be pronounced as "Sah lee day." As it was laid out in 1881, the town's founders boasted of having "within sight of the doors every cottage...10 mountains that raise their hoary peaks hundreds of feet nearer Heaven than does proud old Pike, the sentinel of the plains."

For bike repairs in Salida, try the Tenderfoot Mountain Cyclery at 404 E. Highway 50, 13th and C Street, which is opposite the green road marker for Methodist Mountain along Highway 50.

39

Average highs during the summer range around 84 degrees, with 112 days for growing. Quite a contrast to Silverton!

While in town, you might ride up Spiral Drive to Tenderfoot Hill, recognized by the 'S' on its side. To reach it, turn off CO 291 north of the city limits on County Road 153, and then turn onto County Road 175.

If you're here in June, you will be just in time to watch the FIBA annual kayak race. This began as a 56 mile race down the Arkansas River from Salida to Canon City. Now it's the oldest organized whitewater kayaking event in North America and has been shortened to 26 miles in Salida.

That same weekend in June is the FIBA Citizens' 30 kilometer bicycle race along with a 10 kilometer foot race.

For more fun then, be sure to watch the annual Hooligan Race featuring anything that will float downriver—except a boat.

From Salida to the Royal Gorge, you ride along the Arkansas River through many sharply tilted red rock formations. You pass several cafes and motels along the route along with several campgrounds: Sugarbush 13 miles from Salida; Rivers Edge Campground 14 miles east of Salida;

Red rocks outside Salida

Lake Campground 21 miles east; and KOA 24 miles east.

40 miles out of town you come to the Five Points Recreation area where you can picnic.

47 miles east, you come to the western access to the Royal Gorge at Parkdale. Turn right here, and 5 miles from the turnoff you begin climbing up a narrow winding road for 2.3 miles before arriving at the lookout point. From here you drop down to cross over the Royal Gorge Bridge.

This bridge is the world's highest suspension bridge, built 1055 feet above the Arkansas River. The area also boasts the world's steepest incline railway. For another different view, you can ride the half mile Aerial Tram to glide 1200 feet over the river. You can also take a ride on the Royal Gorge Scenic Railway narrow gauge train. This train offers a 30-minute, 3-mile-long ride.

Unbelievable as it sounds, many kayaks ride the white waters through this incredible canyon. If you want to take a ride, contact the Royal Gorge Rafting headquarters located .5 mile east of the entrance to the Royal Gorge, or call 275-5161.

To view gorge from river, take the finicular ride to bottom

41

Geologists estimate that nature worked for 3 million years to create the Royal Gorge and is still working on it, whittling away at the chasm at the rate of 2 inches each thousand years. Although not as deep or as wide as the Grand Canyon, this gorge was cut through solid granite.

The bridge is considered to be one of the 4 more important suspension bridges built in the U.S., spanning one of the longest rivers in America. It was built in 1929 for $350,000 and was only 6 months under construction without a single fatality. The wire used in the bridge would reach from Denver to New York City, and the structure will support in excess of 2 million pounds—a comforting thought as you cross.

Royal Gorge

The countryside around the Royal Gorge is proving to be one of the richest deposits of prehistoric dinosaur fossil beds in the world. The Museum Range north of Canyon City is very rich in fossils and some of the best specimens found here are being sent to the Smithsonian Institute.

Another rich deposit was found a few miles from the rim of the Royal Gorge, and scientists are working to dig out the remains of giant lizards which roamed this region 7 million years ago. One skeleton, Camerasaurus Supremas, was over 100 feet in length and weighed in excess of 60 tons!

As you leave the area, watch for much feldspar, mica, and beryl along the roadside.

A short distance from the Royal Gorge on your way towards Canon City, you pass Buckskin Joe, the most filmed boom town outside of Hollywood. Films shot here include "Cat Ballou," "The Dutchess and the Dirtwater Fox," "How the West Was Won," and "True Grit."

The town has the actual store owned by H.A.W. Tabor who once served as the postmaster of Buckskin Joe, and who later became a U.S. Senator. Tabor is better known as the man who went from rags to riches back to rags, making 15 million dollars in 15 years, only to lose almost all of it when the price of silver plummeted.

Each authentic structure in Buckskin Joe was selected to match a real building that once stood in the original boomtown of Buckskin Joe. Each building was brought here from various old mining towns around the Colorado mountains to indicate just what a frontier town of 1859 looked like.

To ride into this tourist attraction, continue past the first entrance along the road out of the Royal Gorge. This is a dirt road of 1 mile and is tough riding on a bicycle. Instead, continue along the paved road to the next entrance by the Petting Zoo and turn left. Admission is charged.

There are 2 campgrounds along the road out of the Royal Gorge: KOA located 4 miles from the bridge, and another one 1 mile further.

For a good overlook of the town from 800 feet up, take Skyline Drive, a city-owned paved road which ascends to the top of the hogbacks.

Near Canon City, you can visit Red Canyons Park: 500

acres of unusual rock formations; or the Temple Canyon Park, 640 acres in the mountains. Indian Springs is considered to be one of the richest fossil areas in the world.

Alferd Packer was sentenced here to hang for eating 5 of the 7 "Dimmycrats in Hinsdale County," thereby reducing the "Dimmycratic populayshun of the State." Packer is said to have remarked at his trial, "Of all the meat I've ever eaten, I've found the breast of man the sweetest I've ever tasted."

Places to stay include: Pioneer Motel (275-3015); AAA Motel (275-3319); Sky Valley Motel (275-2783); Royal Gorge Motel; Best Western (275-3377); and the Ramada Inn (275-8676).

The ride to Colorado Springs along Highway 115 is a beautiful 4 lane, divided highway with a good riding shoulder. Though hot at first, the road soon climbs into a forested area and definitely becomes more scenic.

1 mile past the cloverleaf, you come to the Wagon Wheel Campground with food at Mr. C's restaurant.

20 miles further: a BBQ.

23 miles: Sunview Campground.

25 miles: National Museum and Golden Eagle Campground.

28 miles: Fort Carson. Here the road becomes divided again.

Riding into Colorado Springs, you could easily spend several days exploring the various sights here. Probably the most famous is a ride up the Pikes Peak Cog Railway—the world's highest railroad which takes visitors to the 14,110 foot summit. Reservations are suggested: 685-5401. It operates from May through October.

The Mt. Manitou Incline, the world's longest scenic cable railroad, rises from 6,400 feet to 8,600 feet every half hour, pulling up a 68 percent grade. There is hiking from the top as well as a snack bar and picnic facilities. The incline is located on Ruxton Avenue west of Manitou Springs, across from the Pikes Peak Cog Railroad Depot. It operates May through September, with an evening Sequin Trip to overlook the city lights 3,000 feet below in July and August. For reservations, call 685-9086.

Manitou Springs was originally the site of more than 20 mineral springs. The Indians who roamed the area called it the "good medicine ground," and brought their sick and aged to drink from its healthful waters.

Seven Falls is quite spectacular, especially early in June when the water is still plentiful. The canyon is illuminated at night from mid-May to mid-September.

Also you might be interested in visiting the Manitou Cliff Dwellings Museum and Phantom Cliff Canyon, an outdoor museum of Cliff Dwellings and artifacts from the Southwest. Admission is charged.

Santa's Workshop, North Pole, is located near the Cheyenne Mountain Zoo, both interesting spots to visit.

The Cave of the Winds, with its constant temperature of 54 to 56 degrees, is a great place to cool off on a hot summer day. It's located 16 miles west of Colorado Springs on US 24. A guided tour of 40 minutes leaves every 15 minutes. On your way into the Cave, you pass through Williams Canyon, often referred to as the "Baby Grand of Colorado."

Campgrounds in Colorado Springs include one in the Garden of the Gods; Pikes Peak Campground in Manitou Springs; Peak View Campground in town; and the Thunderbird of the Royal Gorge located on US 50 and the Royal Gorge Road.

On July 4th, the annual Pikes Peak Auto Climb is held, a race to the clouds. In August, you can see the Pikes Peak or Bust Rodeo, or the Broadmoor Ice Review.

Colorado Springs is so large with so many motels available that none will be mentioned here.

For bike repairs, try Central Schwinn, 1525 N. University or on S. 8th St.; Ted's Bicycles, 829 N. Tejon; Sollo's Bike Shop at 2641 E. Williamette Avenue; or the Bike Rack, 4735 Flintridge St.

To leave Colorado Springs and avoid I-25 where bicycles are prohibited, cycle east from town to Highway 83. Proceed north along this rolling road for 34 miles to Franktown through forested areas and along a lightly traveled road.

1 mile north of Franktown, you pass a roadhouse; 3 miles further, El Valley Restaurant and a Barn Store; and 4 miles further is the Emerald Isle Grocery Store.

Continuing on towards Parker, you are treated to a bike path the rest of the way to the southern edge of Denver. If you continue north on Parker Road upon reaching Denver, this becomes Leetsdale Drive. To reach Stapleton Airport, stay on Leetsdale Drive until it intercepts Havanna Street and cycle north to 6th Avenue. Turn east and ride to Peoria. Turn north onto Peoria and ride to Montview Blvd. Turn west and cycle to Quebec which leads you directly to Stapleton.

To return to Boulder, follow Quebec to Rosemary. Follow Rosemary to 88th Avenue and cycle through Thornton. Watch for Huron and turn north to ride to 92nd. Follow 92nd to Old Wadsworth and turn west to ride along a wide shoulder to Broomfield.

Once in Broomfield, turn north onto Highway 287 until coming to Highway 128 heading for Jefferson County Airport. Follow 128 along another nice shoulder to Highway 93. Turn north one last time and you're only 4 miles from town.

CENTRAL COLORADO

Distance Traveled

Boulder—Golden	17
Golden—Idaho Springs	20
Idaho Springs—Dillon	39
Dillon—Fairplay	56
Fairplay—Buena Vista	35
Buena Vista—Poncha Springs	21
Poncha Springs—Gunnison	60
Gunnison—Black Canyon	83
Black Canyon round trip	20
Black Canyon—Sapinero	29
Sapinero—Hotchkiss	52
Hotchkiss—Carbondale	68
Carbondale—Aspen	31
Aspen—Leadville	59
Leadville—Dillon	33
Dillon—Boulder	76
	700

Elevation Gain

Boulder—Loveland Pass	6562
Breckenridge—Hoosier Pass	1938
Copper Mt.—Fremont Pass	1638
Denver—Kenosha Pass	4721
Buena Vista—Monarch	3512
Hwy. 50—Black Canyon	2580
Hotchkiss—McClure Pass	3404
Aspen—Independence Pass	4187
Leadville—Tennessee Pass	272
Vail—Vail Pass	2453
Dillon—Loveland Pass	2836

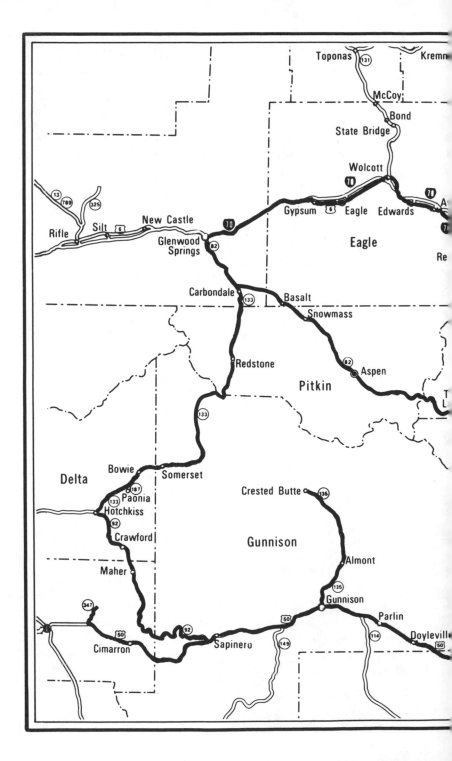

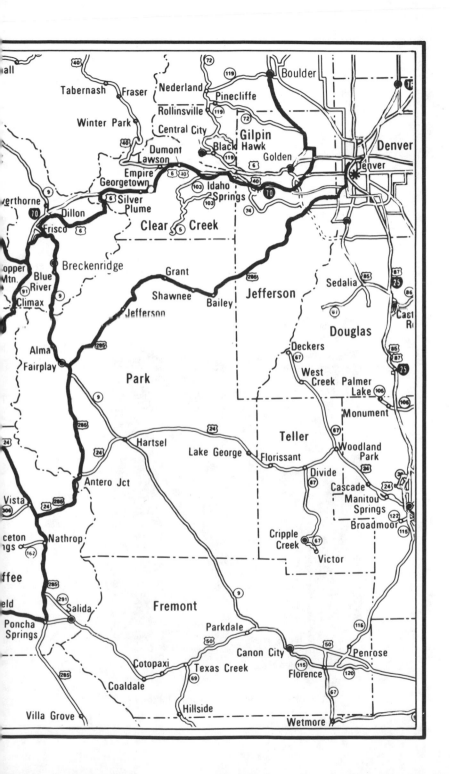

Author's husband at American Lake

Central Colorado

There are 3 possible routes to Buena Vista from the Denver-Boulder area. One is via Highway 93 out of Boulder through Golden, and climbing up through Georgetown over Loveland Pass and dropping down over Highway 9 where you climb Hoosier Pass before arriving in Buena Vista.

The second route is out of Denver via Highway 285 through Morrison and over Kenosha Pass, Red Hill Pass, Trout Creek Pass into Buena Vista.

The third route follows the route over Loveland Pass as far as Frisco and then, instead of following Highway 9, continues on to the Copper Mountain ski area to cross over Fremont Pass (Highway 91) and through the historic silver boom town of Leadville into Buena Vista.

The first route described begins in Boulder. You cycle south on Highway 93 to reach Golden. Caution should be used on this road since once you reach the top of the long hill, the road narrows, offering no shoulder for riding. The road is generally level until crossing Highway 72 when it drops down and becomes a roller coaster road the rest of the way. Very heavy truck traffic begins on this stretch of the road, so be ready to leave the road when 2 trucks approach you from opposite directions.

2 miles north of Golden you pass the turnoff to Golden Gate Canyon, once the shortest route available to the gold miners seeking their fortunes in the gold camps of Black Hawk and Central City to the west.

Golden itself offers several interesting places to visit including the Colorado Railroad Museum located 1 mile east of town. To reach it, turn east from Washington Avenue onto 10th Avenue right next to the city park. The museum is open 7 days a week.

Thirsty cyclists should be sure to visit Coors Brewery on 13th and Ford, for a free tour, including an ample sample.

Rock hounds will certainly enjoy the Colorado School of Mines Geology Museum at 16th and Maple to see one of the state's finest rock collections.

Golden has 2 bike shops. The Pack 'N Pedal is located at 11th and Washington. The other shop is 1 block south on 12th and Walnut, The Golden Bicycle Works.

To leave Golden, cycle south on Washington Avenue to 19th Avenue and turn right. After 1 mile, you will meet Highway 6. From here you have 2 choices: either cycle to Mt. Vernon Canyon and turn west, or take a side trip up Lookout Mountain to visit Buffalo Bill's grave.

To go to the grave, cross Highway 6 at the light and continue west—straight ahead—climbing 2600 feet in 10 miles. Cody was probably one of the most well known of the western scouts, riding for the Pony Express and organizing buffalo hunts for foreign royalty. He also toured the United States and Europe with his wild west show.

While there, you can stop for a picnic in the nearby park, or purchase a snack at the Cody Inn Restaurant in the shopping center west of the grave. Jefferson County Conference and Nature Center is a short distance away from the grave at 900 Colorow Road. This 110 acre site has 1.5 miles of self-guiding trails as well as a mansion that was built in 1917 and is now open for tours.

From the gravesite, continue west along Lookout Mountain Blvd. to intercept Mt. Vernon Canyon Road, Highway 40.

If you choose not to add this additional climb to your trip, upon reaching the light at 19th Avenue and Highway 6, turn left and ride east for a short distance to the next traffic light. Turn right at the light to ride a short stretch along

Highway 93 to where it rejoins Highway 6 just below Heritage Square.

Turn right onto Highway 6 and continue 2 more miles to the next traffic light. Turn west to pick up the Mt. Vernon Canyon Road, Highway 40. This road is not heavily traveled and climbs for 6 miles past some beautiful homes until you must leave it to ride along the Interstate at Exit 254: Genessee Park. Ride along the right hand shoulder of the Interstate for 2 miles, bypassing the exit to Chief Hosa, and continue on to Exit 242 for El Rancho.

Turn right and cross over the Interstate by the El Rancho, a great snacking place with delicious cinammon rolls, and pick up Highway 40 again. Once more you will have a nice road for bicycling until you come down off Floyd Hill and must rejoin the Interstate. Here you ride along the right shoulder until you reach Exit 243 for Hidden Valley after 1.3 miles. Now you ride along another frontage road. You will have to ride the short stretch of dirt (approximately 1 mile), but then you are back on asphalt the rest of the way. Be sure to take this left turn onto the dirt, since the asphalt road crossing the bridge isn't part of the frontage road.

East of Idaho Springs, you will cross over the Interstate to ride through town into their business district.

While here, some points of interest include the Argo Mine and Mill. A long tunnel of 5 miles was drilled 2,000 feet beneath the overlying mountains to reach the many mines in the Central City area. The mine is open for touring from May to September from 9 to 7 daily for an entrance fee.

To ease your riding muscles, stop at the Indian Springs Resort Motel which offers both lodging and hot mineral baths. Other motels in the area include: the Argo Motor Inn (567-4473); Blair Motel (567-2077); H & H Motel (567-2838); or the Krenzel Motel (567-2494).

Good eating spots include Beau Jo's, the Golddigger Restaurant, Sandwich Mines, or the Sugar Plum.

For both a scenic and historic side trip, continue through town 1.5 miles to the Fall River Road, Exit 238, to cycle 9.3 miles up to 10,500 feet to reach both St. Mary's Glacier and Lodge as well as the ghost town of Alice. You will encounter a .1 mile dirt stretch along the road which also has several steep switchbacks as you leave the valley.

Alice is located just below the trail to St. Mary's Glacier on the left hand side of the road. In 1881, Alice was a colony tent site housing many hopeful silver miners. A mill built in 1908 operated until 1915, and the town was the only one in the state to have its own glory hole located within the city limits.

You can buy a good meal at the Silver Lake Inn open Wednesday through Sunday from 12 to 6. The Silver Lake Lodge offers tackle, bait, equipment, and licenses for anyone desiring to fish in the lake. Lodging is also available at Silver Lake either in cabins or condos. Call 567-2865 for reservations.

You can also hike up to St. Mary's Glacier where some avid ski afficianados ski all summer long. The lake is a great picnic or camping area with limited supplies available at the Silver Lake Inn.

Another side trip out of Idaho Springs is up Mt. Evans. To ride up the highest auto road in the U.S., take Exit 103 and climb for 13 miles to Echo Lake at 10,400 feet. For camping along the route, you pass an RV campground, Cottonwood Campground located 1 mile from town, and Pine Crest, 2 miles further up. Otherwise, there are no easily

Remains of town of Alice on St. Mary's Glacier Road

accessible campgrounds until reaching the one at Echo Lake. You do pass a turn off to the Chicago Creek Campground along the way, but it is off the main road and up 3 miles of dirt.

You do pass a couple of picnic grounds: Chicago Forks 8 miles from town, and Ponderosa Picnic area, 10 miles up.

The last few miles below Echo Lake are along some very steep switchbacks and are quite a pull.

At Echo Lake there is a small cafe along with good fishing in the lake. The campground only has 18 sites, so if you're planning to camp, try to arrive as early as possible.

The ride up to the summit of Mt. Evans is a good workout of 14.2 miles with an elevation gain of approximately 4,000 feet. The first 9 miles up to Summit Lake at 12,830 feet are not as steep, but once you pass the lake, you begin to climb very steeply for 5 more miles. Summit elevation is 14,264 feet.

The summit has an observatory, and until a fire in 1970, had a shelter house and snack bar, but now there's nothing left. Be prepared for the inevitable cold and good chance of rain, along with your own supply of water and food. At 14,000 feet, the air is very cool, even on the best days, and you can generally count on the wind's blowing. I would advise your planning to be on top before noon since summer thunderstorms each afternoon are more the rule than the exception.

To make a loop ride back to Idaho Springs, coast down to Echo Lake, making sure your brakes are in excellent working order, and exercising caution along the usually highly eroded road near the top. Continue east along Highway 103 where you will climb back up to 11,200 feet, a gain of another 800 feet in .5 miles, before continuing your descent. Once back in Bergen Park, you'll come to a store for purchasing snacks before continuing on to the El Rancho. From here, retrace your original route to Idaho Springs.

After you've completed your sightseeing in Idaho Springs, continue on towards Georgetown via the frontage road. This road will cross over the Interstate 3 times before reaching Georgetown, and is the site of an annual foot race each August. Aren't you glad you're cycling it rather than running it, even though the runners are "treated" to a slightly downhill run by beginning in Georgetown?

House in Georgetown

As you cycle past Dumont, you're passing what was once old Mill City which still has an old log building built in 1868. It served as an old stage station when the only road along Clear Creek was up the old toll road.

Georgetown was named for George Griffith, who with his brother, staked a claim on Mill Creek. Soon a camp was established called George's Town. The mines there produced over $200 million in gold, silver, copper, and lead during the 33 years that the camp boomed. Some people feel that if the Sherman Act hadn't been repealed in 1893, it could have given Denver a run for its money in population.

In Georgetown, there are several historic sites to visit including the old Hammill House constructed in 1880 and the old Hotel de Paris, built in 1875.

Try to make time to ride the Georgetown-Silver Plume narrow gauge. When the loop was completed in 1882, it became known all over the country as a "must" vacation along with Niagara Falls and Yellowstone National Park. At that time, the long trains brought as many as 25 to 30 carloads of passengers a day to Silver Plume.

The tracks loop back on themselves several times as they climb 600 feet out of the valley before proceeding on to

Silver Plume, another old silver mining town. Here you can get a snack at the Plume Saloon before returning to Georgetown. Granite obtained from Silver Plume was used in constructing the state capitol. In fact, this granite was so hard it was in much demand for the hard rock drilling contests held by the early hard rock miners. For information, call 569-2403 or 569-2788.

Places to stay in Georgetown include the Alpine Inn Lodge at Georgetown (569-3211); Swiss Inn (869-2931); or the Georgetown Motor Inn (569-3201). Places to eat include the Swiss Inn, Wiffletree, Los Dos Mujeres, or the old Chicago Spaghetti and Pizza Company.

Now the climb really becomes steep. Leaving Georgetown via the right hand shoulder of I-70, you cycle for 5 miles to Silver Plume where you exit at #226 and ride along the frontage road for 4.3 miles to Bakerville. Here you once again cycle along the shoulder of I-70 for 5.1 miles until you reach the exit for Loveland Pass via Highway 6.

From this point on, the climb is breathtaking, ascending to an elevation of 11,992 feet. Once on top, if you have the time and energy, why not take a few minutes to look around and perhaps explore one of the trails along the alpine tundra. There's one on either side of the road, giving you a chance to look around at the beauty you might have missed while you were grinding up the pass.

You'll probably need to don a windbreaker for your long descent into Dillon, passing the Arapahoe Basin ski area, and later Keystone ski area. Keystone's resort offers luxurious lodging and meals. Here you can ride the chairlift up Peru Creek from 1 to 3 P.M. Signs have been posted along the lift towers explaining the local history. Once at the top of the lift, you can hike up to the summit house at 11,640 feet. If you want an elegant picnic, order one in advance through the Keystone Sports desk.

Places to eat west of Keystone include the Snake River Saloon and the Bavarian Restaurant.

Campgrounds here include the Tenderfoot Campground at 9156 feet located 6 miles east of Dillon; Prospector Campground, 3 miles east of Dillon and then 3 miles southwest along Highway 91; the Snake River Campground, 6 miles east of Dillon on Highway 6; and Heaton Bay Campground on Dillon Reservoir, 3 miles southwest of town along the dam road.

Motels in the Dillon area include Best Western Ptarmigan (468-2341); Holiday Inn at Lake Dillon (668-5000); Lake Dillon Condotel (468-2409); Ramada Silverthorne at Lake Dillon (468-6200); and Snowshoe Motel (668-3444).

Places to eat include the Bully Three, Arthur Treacher's Fish and Chips, Tappan House, McDonalds, Pug Ryans—all of which are in Dillon—and the Village House of Pancakes and the Ramada Inn Restaurant at Silverthorne.

Dillon has a bike shop located at the stop light by the entrance to town at the Summit Ski Rental shop.

From Dillon, cycle along the dam road on the west side of Lake Dillon towards Frisco. This road offers you a good riding shoulder once you've crossed over the dam. As you approach Frisco, you have access to several other campgrounds: Frisco Marina, 1 mile east of town on county road 9; Sentinel Island .5 mile east of Frisco on US 6; Frisco Bay, 1 mile east of Frisco on Highway 9; Windy Point, 6 miles east of Dillon on US 6; Officer's Gulch, 10 miles southwest of Dillon on Highway 6; Peak I on Dillon Reservoir, 2 miles east of Frisco on Highway 9; and Prospector Campground, 6 miles southeast of Dillon.

Motels in Frisco include the Peak One Motel (668-5666) and Sky Vue Motel (668-3311).

In Frisco, you can either pick up Highway 9 and head for Breckenridge, or follow the bike path paralleling I-70 towards Copper Mountain. If you choose Highway 9, you will soon be treated to a bike path which leads into Breckenridge. Be sure to note the many mounds of rock pilings along the river. This was the result of gold dredges which became about the only way the early miners could do hydraulic mining. The first dredge, built in 1907, floated on the water and used its metal fingers to dig up, wash and screen vast amounts of gold-bearing gravel from the river.

Breckenridge, named after John C. Breckinridge, vice president of the US, was re-spelled after he revealed his favoritism towards the Confederates. The Unionists in town insisted that an "e" instead of the "i" be substituted in his name—a spelling which stuck.

While in town, you can take an alpine slide ride up at the ski area.

Breckenridge has another campground: Tiger Run,

Dredge at Breckenridge

located 3 miles north on SR 9 and then east 1 mile.

Motels in Breckenridge include Beaver Run (456-6000) and Claude's Lodge (453-2420). For central area reservations call 453-2918.

From Breckenridge, the road climbs over Hoosier Pass whose summit is 11,541 feet. The mile just below the summit is the steepest part of the climb. On top you can enjoy a magnificent view of Quandary Peak and Mt. Democrat, two of the state's fourteeners. There is also a rest facility there.

Coast down into Fairplay at 9953 feet where the old historic Fairplay Hotel is located in the center of town. Fairplay was named by Jim Reynolds, a prospector who later became the leader of a group of highwaymen, and made himself boss of the camps, demanding fair play for everyone.

Be sure to watch for the monument erected to Prunes, a burro who lived to the ripe old age of 63. For over 60 years he packed supplies for his mining partner, Rupe. When Rupe was dying, he requested that he be placed in the same grave as Prunes, and his wishes were carried out by the citizens of Fairplay. The monument is located on Front

Street next to the Hand Hotel.

Fairplay also offers the South Park City Museum which is a reconstruction of an early Colorado mining town complete with 22 buildings, many of them original and furnished with authentic items from the past. Open daily from July 1 through Labor Day, admission is charged.

The largest gold dredge in the state operated here, and the courthouse which was built in 1874, is the oldest in the state.

To grab a bite to eat, try the Fairplay Cafe in town, or the Aspen Leaf Restaurant outside of town on Highway 9.

Coming out of Fairplay along Highway 285, you will pass 4 Mile Campground, 6 miles southwest of town. Buffalo Springs Campground is 14.5 miles south of town.

From Antero Junction at 9200 feet you'll climb Trout Creek Pass whose summit is 9346 feet before dropping down into Buena Vista at 7954 feet. Trout Creek was an old Indian trail used when the first Europeans visited the area in 1779. It got its name from the fish found in the streams in the area. However, the miners used up so many of the trees from the surrounding forest that they destroyed the streams' watershed. The low mountains south of the pass are the Arkansas Hills, and the 2 peaks to the north are old volcanoes known as Buffalo Peaks.

Buena Vista, Spanish for beautiful view, is located at the foot of 16 peaks that rise over 14,000 feet, including 3 from the Collegiate Range: Mt. Yale, Mt. Princeton, and Mt. Harvard. Should you decide to stay around here for hiking, you have a wide variety of peaks plus some beautiful valleys and ghost towns to explore. For details on climbing some of these fourteeners, check with the sporting goods stores and pick up a copy of Borneman and Lampert's *Guide to Climbing the Colorado Fourteeners*, as well as a topographical map for Mt. Harvard.

If you decide to ride into Buena Vista via Highway 91 out of Frisco, watch for the bicycling sign, #76, to get onto the bike path that runs along Ten Mile Creek towards Copper Mountain. This path only has a 2-3 percent grade and is 7 miles long with a total elevation gain of 580 feet.

At Copper Mountain, pick up Highway 91 to climb from 9680 feet at Copper to ride to the top of Fremont Pass at 11,318 feet. This pass has a 7 percent grade leading to the

Climax—mountain is being eaten away by miners of molybdenum

top. It was named after John C. Fremont, the great path-finder, who explored much of the area between the Rocky Mountains and the Pacific Ocean during the 1800's. However, it's interesting to note that his expedition never did cross this pass.

Shortly after you reach the top, you will ride through Climax at 11,450 feet, now the site of the largest underground mine in North America with 60 miles of mine openings passing through the extensive ore deposit of molybdenum. During the 1880's, Climax served as a clearing station waypoint for the Denver, South Park, and Pacific Railroad, being named from the railroad station on top of the pass where 2 narrow gauge lines crossed. Molybdenum was discovered there in 1879. It was at first believed to be worthless. Now the mines produce almost half of the world's supply of the ore. 2 hour surface tours are available Monday through Friday starting in mid-June and running through August. They depart at 10 and 1 o'clock, and advance reservations are advised: 486-2150.

There is a picnic area opposite the Climax mine for enjoying a picnic lunch and a great alpine view.

From Climax, you'll enjoy a nice coast down into Lead-

61

ville which at 10,152 feet is the highest incorporated city in the US. Pilots landing at its airport receive a certificate for having landed at the highest airport in the country.

On your way into town, you pass a Lucky 2 Motel (486-0467) and Merlino's Cherry Cider in the shopping center on your right. In Leadville, you can stay in the Best Western Silver King Motor Inn (486-2610); Bel-Air Motel (486-0881); Alps Motel (486-1223); Super 8 Lodge (486-3770); Mountain Peaks Motel (486-3178); or the Timberline Motel (486-1876).

For camping in Leadville, cycle into the center of town and turn west on 6th Avenue to reach the Sugar Loafin' Campground, 3 miles northwest of town.

Places to eat include the Golden Burro Cafe and the Molly Brown Cafe, named after the "Unsinkable Molly Brown" who survived the sinking of the Titanic.

In 1879, Leadville built an impressive ice palace for 35 thousand dollars at a time when the mines in the area were producing 13 million dollars in silver. Pictures of this fantastic palace are on display at the Heritage Museum and Gallery. Incredible as it sounds, mines here have produced over 600 million dollars in gold, silver, lead, and other ores since the rush began in 1877.

Another historical spot to visit here is the Matchless Mine, which was operated by H.A.W. Tabor in 1878. He made a fortune which once equalled over 12 million dollars, and used some of his wealth to build the Tabor Grand Opera House, another interesting site to visit in town. Then, during the silver panic in 1893, all his fortune was lost except for the Matchless Mine which he instructed his wife to hold on to in the event that the price of silver ever made it profitable to operate again. She did so until she froze to death in a cabin near the mine in 1935. The Matchless is open for tours from Memorial Day through Labor Day from 9 to 7.

If time permits, visit the Healy House which was built by James Dexter in 1878, another early billionaire. Here you can view memorabilia from the 1870-80 mining boom era.

For any climbers interested in climbing the state's highest or second highest fourteeners—Elbert and Massive—cycle to the turnoff for Highway 301 outside of Malta, 3 miles west of Leadville. The pavement ends after 1 mile, so you

Road to the Matchless Mine in Leadville

will need to hitch the rest of the 5 miles to Half Moon Campground. The trailhead is located 3.5 miles further, beyond the campground.

Mt. Elbert may also be climbed from the paved Independence Pass road by leaving your bicycles at the Mt. Elbert Lodge several miles above Twin Lakes. Inquire about the trail at the Lodge.

From Leadville, you can enjoy a great coast down Highway 24 into Buena Vista.

The third route to Buena Vista is from Denver. From Stapleton Airport, cycle south on Quebec to Colfax Avenue. Turn east onto Colfax and cycle to Havana, Highway 285. This route bypasses the heart of Denver and turns west onto Hampden. Stay with this highway, continuing on through Morrison and into Conifer.

Soon you will drop hundreds of feet down Crow Hill into Bailey at 7750 feet on the South Platte where the Glen-Isle Resort, Moore-Dale Village, and Stonehenge Ranch offer places to stay.

Shawnee has a store for purchasing picnic supplies and 5 miles beyond Shawnee you pass a motel, store, and restaurant.

Summit of Mt. Elbert—Colorado's highest peak—on first day of summer

6 miles north of Grant, you pass the Burning Bear Campground located on the road that climbs Guanella Pass. In Grant you can stop at the Twin Spruce Restaurant for a bite to eat. For camping, stop at the Kenosha Pass Campground 1 mile below the summit at 10,001 feet.

Dropping back into Jefferson at 9500 feet, you come to the Coronado Motel, Delaney's Depot, and the Three Thieves Restaurant. The road then climbs over Red Hill Pass at 9993 feet before dropping back down into Fairplay at 9953 feet.

From Fairplay, continue as described earlier.

In Buena Vista, you can camp 5 miles north of town along US 24 at the Crazy Horse Camping Resort, or at the KOA Campground on Highway 285, 1.5 miles east of town.

Still another option is the Fisherman's Bridge Campground, 3 miles south on Highway 285.

Motels in Buena Vista include: Alpine Lodge: 395-2415 or Thunder Lodge: 395-2245, and the Jump Steady Motel: 395-6906.

In August, Buena Vista hosts the Buena Vista Triple Crown Burro Race. This consists of 2 contests: one for the contestants and the other for the spectators who try to guess the winning time. The rules of the race are that the burros carry a 35 pound pack containing a gold pan, pick, and shovel and they must be pushed, pulled or somehow gotten through the rugged mountains north of town. However, contestants are not allowed to ride the burros. The winner in 1980 covered the distance in 3 hours 20 minutes, managing to win $1200.

7.5 miles south of town along Highway 285 is the turn off to the Mt. Princeton Hot Springs. There are 2 more campgrounds along this road, Chalk Creek and Mt. Princeton Campground. From Chalk Creek's Campground, you can take a short hike up to Angel Falls.

For those interested in climbing another fourteener, follow the trail up Mt. Princeton. It begins 1 mile west of the hot springs pool. You can either hitch a ride up from there to the Young Life Frontier Camp or hike the full distance.

Antero is also climbed from this area by proceeding beyond the site of the ghost town of Alpine, 2.5 miles west of Highway 285 on the Mt. Princeton Road. Turn left from Alpine to follow a very rough jeep road. You have a large stream to cross part way up, and if you're as lucky as I was, a jeep will come by at just the right moment to take you across.

Continuing south on Highway 285 towards Poncha Springs, the road is very wide and quite enjoyable for cyclists. At Poncha Springs, named for a nearby mine, turn west onto Highway 50 to cross over Monarch Pass which tops out at 11,312 feet, a climb of 3512 feet from Buena Vista. If you've ever seen this road in the winter, you can appreciate the fact that the original roadbed was relocated because it filled up with snow much too quickly. Fortunately, you won't have to worry much about heavy snows during the summer, although it often does snow even then.

Once on top, you may wish to stop and have a snack at

Panoramic view from top of gondola—Monarch Pass

their snack bar, and perhaps ride the gondola to the top of the Continental Divide for a tremendous 360 degree view of the plains to the east and 7 different mountain ranges, many with some of the state's highest fourteeners including Mt. Shavano, Pikes Peak, and Sawatch. The hike to the top is an easy one—only about 1 mile, if you prefer to make it on your own.

Monarch Pass has 2 places for overnighting: The Ramada Inn (539-2581) and the Monarch Motor Lodge (539-6733).

The Monarch Pass Campground is located 14.5 miles west of Poncha Springs and 1 mile south of FR #235 where good fishing is reportedly available.

Now you enjoy a long coast and then a more flat ride from the top of Monarch Pass into Gunnison, a distance of 42 miles.

In Gunnison you can stay at the Crescent Motel (641-1263); Dos Rios Motor Hotel (641-1000); Harmel's Guest Ranch (641-1740); Western Motel (641-1722); Tomichi Village Inn (641-1131); or Holiday Motel (641-0270).

Places to eat include Cattleman's Inn Restaurant, Pizza Hut, Kentucky Fried Chicken, A & W, or the Gunnison Restaurant.

The West Elk Road Club promotes a 3 day bicycle race over the Labor Day week-end. They also sponsor 2 other citizen's bike races later that same month. For information, call the Tune Up Ski and Bike Shop at 641-0285.

For a scenic side trip, why not cycle to Crested Butte, 28 miles from Gunnison and an additional climb up to 8800 feet? This is one of the more scenic ski areas in the state and also affords some great flower viewing.

On your way out of town towards Crested Butte, you pass the Paradise Park Motel (641-2927) and the Shady Island Resort (641-0416), both located along a stream.

North of Almont, you come to another campground and some cabins. You also pass an old cemetery on the right side of the road, Jack's Cabin Cemetery. This gives you an interesting look into the past.

As you approach Crested Butte, you get a fabulous view of the back side of the well known Maroon Bells.

Judd Falls near Gothic

In Crested Butte, you can stay at the Ore Bucket Lodge (349-5519); Crested Butte Lodge (349-5322); Lazy K Resort (641-9901); or the Elk Mountain Lodge (349-5114). The central reservation number for Crested Butte is 349-6601.

For dining out, try the Artichoke Restaurant at the ski area, or the Wooden Nickel, Three Thieves, or Penelope's in Crested Butte.

9 miles above Crested Butte you come to Gothic where there is another campground, Avery Peak Campground. Here you can sleep at a delightfully cool altitude of 8900 feet. The first 4 miles to Gothic are paved, but the last 5 are dirt. However, Gothic is an interesting spot to visit, now serving as the locale for the Rocky Mountain Biological Lab where college students spend the summer studying the wild plants and animals of the area.

Gothic was one of the most important mining camps in the Gunnison area during the 1880's because of its abundance of silver.

After returning to Gunnison, continue west on Highway 50 to visit the Black Canyon of the Gunnison. As you leave town, you pass several other campgrounds, Long Holiday Motel, 1 mile west, and Mesa Campground, 4 miles east.

After 10 miles you reach the beginning of the Blue Mesa Reservoir, which is the largest body of water in the state. After 1 mile of cycling along Blue Mesa you reach Stevens Creek Campground where you can camp along the water's edge and fish; 1 mile further, Sunrise Campground; 4 miles further, Elk Creek Campground; 10 miles, Lake Fork Campground; 3.4 miles from Lake Fork Campground is the Blue Mesa Cafe and Motel.

The road continues to climb to the top of the reservoir before dropping down into a steep canyon and then climbing again to the end of the reservoir where there is a good eating place at the Peaceful Valley Cafe. There are also cabins and another campground here.

Continue along Highway 50, passing Cimmaron, where there is a cafe and motel, and the turnoff for the Morrow Point Dam and an historic park exhibit. Continue up to the top of Cerro Summit and then down to the entrance of the Black Canyon of the Gunnison. There is a cafe, picnic, and rest area located at the intersections of Highway 50 and C 347.

The road into the Black Canyon is a very steep one with 3 cattle guard crossings, but it's paved all the way. After 10 miles of climbing, you reach the fee area. 1 mile further you reach Tomichi Point, a short distance from the monument headquarters.

Literature from the area points out that the Gunnison River started cutting into the rock 2 million years ago, and geologists figure that the gorge has deepened about 1 foot each thousand years. The canyon is approximately 53 miles long, but the deepest and most spectacular section of the rivercut is here in the Black Canyon. Because of its depth, which ranges from 1730 feet to 2700 feet, the sun is only able to penetrate the canyon for short periods of time, hence its name. The elevation along the south rim is approximately 8000 feet, with a high point of 8400 feet. The climb to here is about 2580 feet from Highway 50.

From the headquarters, you can take a 6 mile ride along the south rim and stop at various lookouts. The one at the end of the road offers a hike along the Rim Rock Nature Trail. The path has 14 posts which point out various points of interest as you trek the three quarters of a mile to Tomichi Point.

There are 2 campgrounds in the monument with one located on each rim. However, while the north rim is a gravel road, the campground on the south rim is on a paved road.

After you have taken in all the scenic views of the canyon, cycle back down, again being cautious as you cross the cattle crossings, to Highway 50. At this point, you have a choice to make. You can either turn west and continue on to Montrose, or for a more scenic route, return to Sapinero to cycle up a most scenic road over Black Mesa on Highway 92. This road was a real find for me, since it travels above the Gunnison River many feet below, while winding through many beautiful miles of forested land.

The road, though scenic, is a tough climb. If strong winds are blowing, it can provide a real challenge, but the view makes it definitely worth your time. There aren't any campgrounds along the first part of this route, although there is a pullout along the way where you can stop to look down over the valley below your feet. The road continues for 61 miles to a campground located by the lake at Craw-

Overlook from Black Mesa Road

ford Reservoir. 2 miles farther on, you reach Crawford where I saw no motel, but did see some places to eat: Silver Dollar Diner and Lounge, Boardwalk Restaurant, and the Wagon Wheel Grill. Crawford Pioneer Park is in the center of town for picnicking.

As you leave town, you can't help but become aware of the volcanically formed mountain off to your right, and another formation closely resembling Shiprock, an old volcanic plug in New Mexico, visible from Mesa Verde's road.

Continue on towards Hotchkiss, 11 miles beyond Crawford, where you can find motels such as the Quarter Circle Motel (872-3266) and the Douglas Motel (872-3644). For a snack, try the Charlie Brown Drive Inn.

After leaving Hotchkiss, we turned right onto Highway 133 where we passed Winnie's Inn, and continued out of town for 7 more miles to a very nice place to stay overnight: Redwood Arms Motel and Restaurant (527-4148).

After leaving there, we passed the town of Paonia where on July 4th, they celebrate Cherry Days with parades and a hot air balloon. Paonia is the nation's largest coal reserve. Water supplying the town is claimed to be 99.95 percent pure, coming from springs on Mt. Lamborn south of town. Accommodations here may be found at the Rocky Mountain Motel (523-3070).

11 miles from the Redwood Arms is a place to snack— The Portal. Now the road continues to climb gradually beside Paonia Reservoir, and passes many coal mines. As you approach McClure's Pass, whose summit is 8755 feet, you'll encounter 3 miles of hard packed dirt which has one short, steep hill to climb before it levels out somewhat and becomes paved once again. In 1980, they were constructing a new road to replace this dirt stretch.

There is a very nice campground before McClure's Pass: McClure Campground. Then 6 miles beyond here, you come to the turn-off to Marble where there is another campground.

The road into Marble is dirt, but if you can finagle a ride into town, a jeep will take you the remaining distance to tour the old mine which provided marble for such structures as the Jefferson and Washington Memorials in Washington, D.C., as well as for the Colorado National Bank and Colorado State Museum in Denver. The block of marble used for the Tomb of the Unknown Soldier weighed 55 tons and took over a year to remove from the quarry.

After you come off McClure's Pass, you have a very scenic coast into Redstone. Be sure to stop near the bottom of the pass and see Hays Creek Falls.

Redstone is a definite tourist attraction. Watch for the old coke ovens along the side of the road prior to the intersection to Redstone. These ovens were constructed in the late 1890's to carbonize coke coal. The coke was then shipped to Pueblo via the Crystal River Railroad.

In Redstone, you can stay in the Redstone Inn (963-2527) which is open year-round. Between Redstone and Carbondale are several more motels: Crystal Valley Manor (963-2365) or Redstone Cliffs which has kitchen facilities (963-2691). You'll pass a grocery store in Redstone, or you can eat at the Town House.

If you prefer to camp, a campground is 1 mile out of town. 5 miles further is another campground: BRB Campground and Motel (963-2341).

From Redstone, return to Highway 133 to cycle to Carbondale at 6181 feet. In Carbondale, you can stay at Thunder

River Lodge (963-2543) off Highway 82 and eat at the Italian Restaurant nearby. Be sure to watch for the twin peaked mountain close by: Mt. Sopris.

Now you can have another choice to make. You can either cycle into Glenwood Springs or into Aspen. If you go to Glenwood, 12 miles from Carbondale, you can enjoy a swim in the 2 block long, world's largest warm mineral water swimming pool. Places to stay here include: Frontier Lodge (945-5496); Ponderosa Lodge (945-5058); Caravan Motel (945-7455); Hotel Denver (945-6565); or the Glenwood Hot Springs Lodge (945-6571)—both the latter across from the pool.

Places to eat include the Pizza Inn, Kentucky Fried Chicken or the Smithy Restaurant in the shopping center on the east side of the street as you enter town.

For camping, try Ami's located 1 mile west on North Frontage Road on the north side of I-70, or the Hideout Ltd., located 1 mile south from the center of town on Highway 82 and then one quarter mile west on Grant Avenue and 1 mile south on the Sunlight Ski Road: #117; or Rock Gardens Campground located 100 feet south on the frontage road by I-70.

From Glenwood Springs, you can return to Denver via Glenwood Canyon, but the State Highway Department cautions that the canyon is narrow and curving, with no visibility for the cyclist, and thus can be quite dangerous. However, if you decide to take the route, you can follow a bike route for 1.5 miles from town. To pick it up, cycle north of the swimming pool on 6th Street. Ride easterly, ignoring the deadend sign. Pass the Vapor Caves and slip through an opening in the fence onto the bike path. Parallel I-70 for 1.5 miles to an overpass. Cross to the south side of I-70 and continue along the river being sure to watch for rocks and gravel on the road. Look for a cable that has been stretched across the road .5 mile east of the overpass. Watch for the opening on the left side of the cable where you cross back onto the highway at interchange 119 at Dotsero.

From Dotsero you can either ride the shoulder of the interstate or follow Highway 6 through Gypsum to West Vail.

If you choose to ride into Aspen, either from Carbondale or from Glenwood Springs, you can enjoy a beautiful ride along the river. The road is narrow once you leave Glenwood Springs, but visibility along the route is good.

There are several campgrounds on the way to Aspen: Avalanche Campground in Carbondale; KOA-Aspen-Basalt Campground near Basalt; and several others located on the Ruedi Reservoir, 16 miles east of Basalt: Chapman Dam, Mollie B., Little Maud and Little Mattie.

Best Western Aspenalt Lodge is in Basalt (528-1234).

The ride from Glenwood Springs to Aspen is 42 miles, climbing from 5746 feet to 7908 feet. Aspen also has several campgrounds: Maroon Lake, Silver Bell, Silver Bar and Silver Queen—all up the Maroon Bells road 10 miles southwest of Highway 82. These campgrounds only allow 1 day camping because of their desirable location near the Bells, and no cars are allowed to drive this road unless they are camping.

Difficult Campground, my favorite hangout, is located 4 miles southeast of Aspen on the Independence Pass Road, Highway 82. Other campgrounds on Independence Pass include: Weller, located 8 miles east of town; Lincoln Gulch 10 miles further; and Lost Man Campground, 14 miles up

Maroon Lake

the pass.

Motels in town include the Aspen Inn (925-6300); Apple-jack Inn (925-7650); Alpenblick (925-2260); Bavarian Inn (925-7391); Blue Spruce Lodge (925-3991); Highlands Inn (925-5050); Holiday Inn (925-1500); and Ullr Lodge (925-7696). A central reservations number for Aspen is 925-4000.

Aspen was quite rich in ore deposits with nuggets of incredible size being unearthed there. In 1894, a nugget was found in the Smuggler Mine that weighed 2060 pounds, containing 93 percent silver.

For classical music lovers, be sure to attend a musical concert in the tent provided by the Aspen Music Festival orchestra and choir. Seating inside is expensive, but you can also listen to the concert by sitting outside the tent on the grass.

To visit a reconstructed ghost town, ride up to Ashcroft located 12 miles southwest of town up Castle Creek Road. This turnoff is at the same intersection for the Maroon Bells next to the large church, where you turn left. Ashcroft once rivaled Aspen in size during the 1880's when Aspen was a "dusty, sleepy little hamlet." At that time, you could only reach Ashcroft by crossing over Taylor Pass where it was necessary to lower the wagons piece by piece over a 40 foot drop near the top.

While you're in the area, how about hiking up my favorite trail to American Lake? It's a 1965 foot gain in 3.5 miles and is breathtaking. The trailhead is north of Ashcroft on the right hand side opposite Taylor Pass jeep road. You'll see a parking area where you can leave your bike for your walk through the ponderosa and aspen forest and even do some fossil snail hunting along the lower parts of the trail.

You can also buy an outstanding lunch at the Pine Creek Cook House on the south side of Ashcroft. It's open from 12:30 to 2:30 for lunch and 6:30 to 9 for dinner. Closed Mondays, reservations are highly recommended.

Another day, be sure to ride up to see the Maroon Bells, a ride of 11 miles and an elevation gain of 1600 feet climbing up to 9600 feet. Watch for the 3 cattle guard crossings, all well marked. Once in the parking area, why not take the short hike up the well marked trail to Crater Lake just below the Bells?

American Trail as it leaves the valley to climb through a dense forest

For a break from cycling, take the chairlift at the High-lands Ski area, and after hiking to the top of the nearby peak, you can either ride the chair back down or hike down the service road through some fantastically beautiful wild flowers.

If you've never done any kayaking, here's your chance. Contact Aspen Kayaking at 925-4433 or write P.O. Box 1520A, Aspen, Colorado 81611. They operate from May through August with classes offered daily, weekly, or over the week-end.

Eating in Aspen is a gourmet's delight, and prices vary widely. One of the more inexpensive places to eat is at the Skier's Chalet located at the foot of lift #1. For excellent seafood, eat at the Captain's Anchorage. Other good eateries include Guido's Swiss Inn, The Red Onion, and The Sooper.

After you decide to tear yourself away from Aspen, cycle east on Highway 82 to climb Independence Pass, climbing from 7908 feet to 12,095 feet in 20 miles. Extreme caution should be exercised when riding through the 3 very narrow sections on this pass. Since many recreational vehicles use this pass, there is no room left for the cyclist when two of

Looking east from Independence Pass

them attempt to pass each other from opposite directions. The climb is a very steady one, with some flatter areas below Lost Man Campground. After that, it becomes much steeper.

It's always fun to stop for pictures at the old ghost town of Independence located just above treeline. Built in 1879 after a big strike on July 4th, the town once had 800 residents during the time it flourished both as a mining camp as well as a stage stop between Aspen and Leadville. Just imagine: bed and board was available for 75 cents along with oats for your horse for just 10 cents.

Above Independence, the steepest part of the climb is still ahead of you, and you can see the road climbing steadily out of the valley without the aid of any switchbacks. It always looks steeper than it is, but it is a pretty good grind, particularly after you turn east and have to climb still one more steep but short stretch to reach the summit.

As you pedal up, you might find it interesting to contemplate what the pass must have looked like when it was all boulders and huge drop-offs, complete with toll bridges installed every 3-4 miles along the route. Each bridge was only wide enough for one animal or one man to cross, and cost 25 cents every time you crossed it. Early newspaper accounts report that the worst part of this pass was the steep descent from the summit into Independence.

Originally, the top of the pass itself was so narrow that if 2 wagon drivers met there, it was traditional for them to have a fist fight with the loser having to drive off into the mud and give way.

Once you've achieved the summit, stop to have your picture taken by the sign and dabble your hand in the icy waters of the lake. If you're still overheated, you can probably find some snow for a snowball fight, even in the middle of summer.

This pass just misses being the highest continuous paved road in the Rockies, right behind Trail Ridge's high point at 12,183 feet.

The coast down into Twin Lakes is a nice long one of 38 miles, losing 2885 feet down to 9210 feet. 3 miles west of Twin Lakes you pass another beautiful campground: Parry Peak.

Also there are accommodations available at Twin Lakes at the Mt. Elbert Lodge, and in the Twin Lake Olsen Cottages, as well as a motel located at the intersection of Highways 82 and 24.

Depending upon your time and remaining energy, you can either return to the Denver area by backtracking over Highway 91 to Climax and return via Loveland Pass, or for a different route, cycle to Leadville and then follow Highway 24 to Redcliff to cross over Tennessee Pass at 10,424 feet and then dropping down into Minturn.

Tennessee Pass's east side is relatively gentle while the west side has steep canyons where the state's most impressive highway bridge is located outside of Redcliff. The pass crosses the Continental Divide between the Tennessee fork of the Arkansas (named by homesick prospectors in the 1860's) and the Eagle River. It was the first divide crossing to be kept open in the winter starting in 1928. Prior to that, residents of western Colorado either took the train crossing the pass or stayed home between December and May.

At the top of the pass is a memorial to the 993 members of the 10th Mt. Division killed in action in World War II. West of the pass is Camp Hale, which during the war, was an important training center for the ski-equipped soldiers. Many of them returned from the war to become the originators of the Aspen ski boom.

Between the above mentioned bridge and Minturn is a long climb up to the summit of Battle Mountain.

There are 2 campgrounds at Minturn: Hornsilver located 9.5 miles southeast of town, and Homestake, closer to town.

If you're a hiker in search of still another fourteener, you are close to the trailhead for Mt. of the Holy Cross, 14,055 feet. The trail starts up the dirt road leading to Tigiwon Campground 2 miles south of Minturn and 6 miles further up via more rough dirt. From there you need to travel 2 more miles to Campground Half Moon, so hope for a nice pickup truck coming out of Minturn.

Continuing on towards I-70, you will need to cycle along its right hand shoulder for 2 miles to reach West Vail where you can get off and cross over to the north side of I-70 to ride along the frontage road into Vail 2.5 miles further down the road.

Motels in Vail include: Christiana at Vail (476-2261); Kiandra Lodge (476-5081); Lodge at Vail (476-5011); Rams Horn Lodge (476-5646); Talisman Lodge (476-5763); Vail Village Inn (476-5622); and Valhalla at Vail (476-5641).

From Vail you can follow the frontage road along the south side of the Interstate, continuing past Interchange #180 and crossing under I-70 to the Gore Creek Campground.

You'll now be treated to a newly constructed bike path all the way over the pass including a short 14 percent grade. The pull continues past Black Lakes, another good camping spot, up to the Vail Pass rest area at 10,603 feet, an elevation gain of 2453 feet from Vail.

Be careful on the descent as the path has a tendency to be sandy. Once at the bottom of the pass, cycle through the Copper Mountain parking lot and cross Highway 91 to pick up another bike path. Turn left and enjoy a 7 mile coast along Ten Mile Creek to Frisco and return to Denver via Loveland Pass and your original route.

NORTHERN COLORADO

Distance Traveled

Boulder—Estes 38
Estes—Grand Lake 40
Grand Lake—Granby 16
Granby—Kremmling 27
Kremmling—Steamboat Springs 52
*Steamboat—Tonopas 31
Tonopas—Kremmling 35
Kremmling—Granby 27
Granby—Boulder 110
                                             376

*Alternate route
Tonopas—Wolcott 34
Wolcott—Vail 15
Vail—Golden 111
Golden—Boulder 17
                                             381

Elevation Gain

Boulder—Estes 2092
Estes—Trail Ridge 4661
Kremmling—Rabbit Ears 2062
Tonopas—Gore Pass 1247
Kremmling—Berthoud Pass 3950
Dillon—Loveland Pass 2836

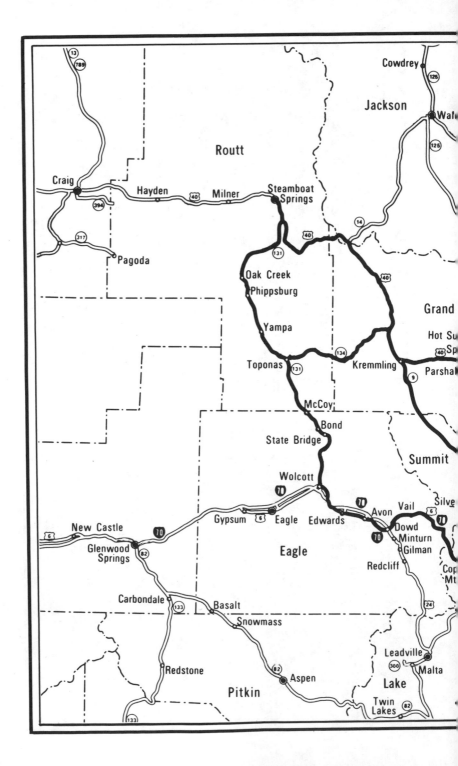

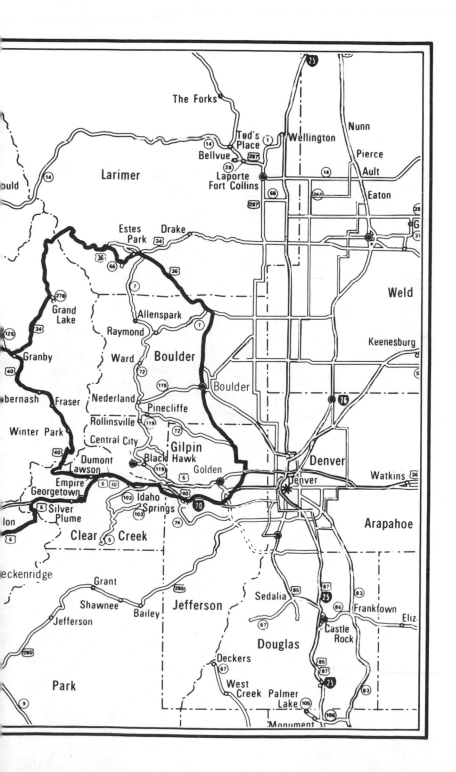

Bike repairs on Trail Ridge. Be sure to keep anything tied onto the rack from getting caught in your spokes or derailleurs! Tube and tire were both trashed out.

Northern Colorado

From Boulder, cycle north to Lyons along the wide shoulder most of the way along Highway 36, Foothills Highway. Just outside of Lyons at the intersection with Highway 66, turn left to cycle into town. Once through Lyons, continue to follow Highway 36 up North St. Vrain Canyon to Estes Park.

The ride up the canyon is fairly flat at first, but begins to steepen just below Pinewood Springs. After that, the road climbs more gradually for 9 more miles before descending for 2.6 miles into Estes Park. Distance to here is 36 miles, with Estes Park's elevation at 7522 feet.

In Estes, there are several places for camping: Aspenglen Campground located at the Fall River entrance 5 miles west of town on U.S. 34, Trail Ridge Road; Moraine Park Campground, 7 miles west of town via Highway 66 to the Beaver Meadows entrance and then along the Bear Lake Road; and Glacier Basin located on the Bear Lake Road 9 miles southwest of town. Both the latter campgrounds require a reservation which can either be made in advance by calling 586-2391 or at the park headquarters prior to riding into the campground. Campsites are assigned.

If these campgrounds are all full, there are several commercial campgrounds outside of the park, at either the northern or southern entrances.

Bear Lake in Rocky Mountain Park on right side backed by snow covered peaks

For motels, there's Anderson's Wonderview Cottages (586-4158); Aspen Lodge and Guest Ranch (387-4241); Best Western Lake Estes Motor Inn (586-3386); Brynwood on the River (586-3476); Castle Mountain Lodge (586-3664); Estes Village Motor Inn (586-5338); Fall River Motor Inn (586-4116); Holiday Inn (586-2332); or the Timberlane Motor Lodge (586-3137).

For eating out, try the Black Canyon Restaurant, the Edel Haus, Holiday Inn's restaurant, or the Lazy B Ranch-Chuckwagon Supper.

If you arrive in town during the Coors Bicycle Classic held during the early part of the summer, you'll be able to watch the criterium for the racers in the center of town.

The ride over Trail Ridge via Highway 34 is a very strenuous one, and one which should be started early enough in the day so that you can be on top by noon to avoid the usual afternoon thunderstorms and lightning. Once you get above timberline, you also pick up more wind, with average speeds ranging from 15 to 30 miles per hour.

This road is reached by cycling through town and turning left at the traffic light in the center of town. Ride to the entrance of Rocky Mountain Park where there is a small fee charged for bicyclists (50 cents per person in 1980).

From here you begin the steady 20 mile climb to the top, passing through a pine forest to the spectacular alpine tundra. Be sure to watch for the Mummy Range off on the north side of the road, and Long's Peak (14,256 feet) off on the south, easily identifiable by its large flat top.

You pass through Rock Cut to climb the last few hundred feet to the summit at 12,183 feet before dropping down to the Alpine Visitor's Center.

At this center you can purchase a hot meal to tide you over for the delightful descent into Grand Lake.

It's 40 miles from Estes to Grand Lake where you can stay in one of the following places: Spirit Lake Lodge (627-3344); Bromhurst Cottages (627-3410); Lemmon Lodge (627-3314); Driftwood Lodge (627-3654); Western Riviera Motel (627-3580); or the Driftwood Lodge (627-3654).

For eating out in the park, pick up a sandwich from Frivolous Salz. Other places to eat include the Restaurant and Beer Gardens for Mexican cuisine, Spirit Lake Lodge's outdoor beer garden, and the Village Square Restaurant.

Grand Lake, a glacially formed lake which is now the state's largest natural body of water, is renowned as the world's largest yacht anchorage. Now it is connected by canal to two other man-made lakes: Shadow Mountain Reservoir and Lake Granby. These 3 lakes offer good sailing and boating as well as beautiful hiking and fishing.

A good time to arrive in Grand Lake is during the first week in August when the town hosts a week-long regatta for both the Sir Thomas Lipton and Colorado trophies. Also while there, be sure to take a guided boat tour to hear about the fabulous homes fronting the lake.

Campgrounds in the area include: Timber Creek Campground, 10 miles northwest of Grand Lake in Rocky Mountain Park; Mountaineer Campground south of Grand Lake; Green Ridge Campground located at the south end of Shadow Mountain Reservoir, 4.5 miles southwest of Highway 34; Stillwater Campground on Lake Granby, 6.5 miles southwest of Grand Lake; and Arapaho Bay located near Monarch Lake.

For a couple of good eating places along Highway 34 on your way to Granby, which is 18 miles below Grand Lake,

Aerial showing glacially carved valley below steep east face of Longs

Hairpin turns on Trail Ridge climbing out of Estes

try the Silver Tips Inn or the Rustic Lantern.

In Granby, places to stay include: the El Monte with its own restaurant (887-3348); the Broken Arrow (887-3532); Homestead Motel (887-3665); Westerner (887-2093); Thunderbird Motel (887-2331); Frontier Motel (887-3636); Blue Spruce Motel (887-3300); or the Best Vu Park (887-2034).

Two other possible eating places include the Chuckwagon Cafe west of the El Monte, and the Bear's Lair in town.

Granby has a bicycle shop, The Wheeler D'ler, located in the Country Hardware Store on the north side of the street, opposite the Texaco Station.

From Granby, cycle out Highway 40 to Hot Sulphur Springs, 11 miles west. Be sure to notice all the cottonwood trees through here. During the 1870's, these trees had been cut down by the beaver and buffalo, but after the fur trappers got through trapping the animals, the cottonwoods had a chance to return.

Accommodations in Hot Sulphur Springs include: the Ute Trail Motel (725-3326); Canyon Motel (725-3395); Stagecoach Stop Hotel (725-9990); and the Riverside Hotel near the pool (725-9096).

You can also camp in the Pioneer Park Campground opposite the pool.

If time permits, why not stop in for a swim in the barnlike building housing the large pool? Water temperatures range from 105 to 123 degrees.

You will pass another unmarked campground 2 miles west of Hot Sulphur Springs located on the left side of the highway after you've crossed the Colorado River.

Continuing out of town through Byers Canyon, proceed with caution along this narrow, heavily traveled road. You will soon pick up a good riding shoulder once you're outside of Parshall, 5 miles later. This good shoulder will be available almost all the rest of the way into Kremmling.

Kremmling is 600 feet lower than Granby, 27 miles away, and places to stay here include: the Hotel Eastin (724-3261); Bob's Western Motel (724-3266); Blue Valley Cabins (724-3571); Gore View Hotel (724-9971); and the Riviera Motel (627-3580).

There is a city park at 3rd and Park in the center of town close to a supermarket, should you wish to purchase supplies for a picnic.

At this point, I would advise stocking up on plenty of liquid and food to carry you all the way into Steamboat Springs since the next 52 miles are all mountainous, with no towns or water available along the way. In August, 1980, we had counted on refilling our water bottles at one of the campgrounds on Rabbit Ears Pass, but no water was available.

Now for the climb. Continue along Highway 40 where you will encounter a great deal of truck traffic and no shoulder for riding. Whenever two trucks approached me coming from opposite directions, I rode off onto the dirt shoulder.

You climb to the top of Muddy Pass at 8772 feet and then continue climbing to the summit of Rabbit Ears at 9426 feet.

After reaching the top of Rabbit Ears, the road continues to follow some rolling terrain, passing some camping areas including Dumont Lake, 24 miles southeast of Steamboat Springs, and 1.5 miles north on a dirt road. 3 miles further west you come to Walton Creek, and 2 miles beyond here is Meadows Campground. For camping outside of Steamboat Springs, continue to within 1 mile of town to pitch your tent at Fishcreek Campground, along Highway 40.

While in Steamboat, you can enjoy a leisurely swim in their large mineral pool on the east side of town. It's open from noon to 8 all year long. You can also visit some of the other hot springs near the park in the west end of town. These natural hot springs gave the town its name when a French trapper traveling along the Yampa River in 1865 thought he heard the chugging of a steamboat. At one time, there were over 150 hot and cold springs in this area.

For some good cycling side trips, ride up to Clark, an old mining town begun in the 1800's, 18 miles up Highway 129 where you can buy a snack at the general store. If time and energy permit, continue 9 miles further north on this same road to ride to Steamboat Lake.

Another nice loop ride is to ride south out Highway 131 to the first left turn-off. This lightly traveled roller-coaster road goes past the aborted ski resort of Stagecoach before it rejoins Highway 131 at Phippsburg. The round trip is approximately 50 miles.

The ride up Rabbit Ears Pass from the Steamboat Springs side is a steep one of 7 percent grade for over 7 miles before it becomes rolling hills. Fortunately, the pass has a climb lane most of the way, and you'll pass several campgrounds where you can stop for your "moveable feasts", culminating with a final meal on top of the pass (if you haven't already consumed it by then.) The elevation gain is 4,024 feet.

Much good hiking is available in the Steamboat area. For a map of the area, stop by the Chamber of Commerce to pick up their large map of the Routt National Forest.

A short one mile hike may be taken up to Fish Creek Falls, with longer hikes available along this same trail. To reach this trailhead, turn north onto 3rd Street for 1 block and then turn right to follow Fishcreek Falls Road to the trailhead. The first couple of miles of this road are paved, but the last two aren't.

Another hike is up Hahn's Peak off Highway 129 near Steamboat Lake. For more detailed directions, check with one of the sporting shops in town, or call the Parks and Recreation Department at 879-4300.

If you cycle to the ski area, 2.2 miles east of town, you can take a ride on the longest single gondola span in the world, rising 2200 feet to Thunderhead Peak. The gondola operates 9 to 2:30 daily from June to Labor Day.

If you're a racing bicyclist, you might check at the Sore Saddle Bicycle Shop to see if there are any races being held while you're in town.

For any competitive road runners, check with the Inside Edge Sporting Shop for any possible runs that might be scheduled. For a true challenge, run the Mountain Madness Half Marathon in August. It starts in town and winds through the ski area before returning, giving your legs a real workout!

For an unforgettable view of the Steamboat Springs area, consider going for an airplane ride over the valley. For information, call Steamboat Aviation at 879-1204.

If you'd like to take a float trip, contact the Sheraton Steamboat Resort at 879-2220.

Some motels in the area include: the Holiday Inn (879-2250); Anchor Motel (879-0675); Alpiner (879-1430); Ptarmigan

Old cabin at Hahn's Peak out of Steamboat Springs

(879-1730); Iron Horse Inn (879-0340); and Rabbit Ears Motel (879-1150).

Places to eat include the Pine Grove Restaurant, Cameo Restaurant, Good Taste Crepe Shop, Dos Amigos, and the Gold Mine. There are also many good eating spots up at the ski area including the Butcher Shop and the Clocktower Restaurant.

In leaving Steamboat Springs, we decided to cross Gore Pass rather than to continue back out Highway 131 to Wolcott and on to I-70. However, if you prefer this longer route, there is food and accommodations available at Wolcott, and food at Edwards at a truck stop. Vail has many motels available, so none will be listed here.

From Vail, you will be treated to a newly constructed bike path, complete with one 14 percent grade section, to the top of the pass. In 1981, a large rest area was completed where you can refill your water bottles, if necessary.

For camping, Gore Creek Campground is located 3.9 miles west of Vail along the bike path's north side.

From the Copper Mountain ski area, upon reaching the intersection with Highway 91, turn left and continue through the parking area onto a separate bike path which will provide you with total separation from the other vehicular traffic along I-70.

This bikepath paralleling the interstate travels for 7 miles downhill into Frisco where you'll turn right onto US 6 and then left onto Highway 9 to ride through town. To camp out and to reach Dillon, turn right onto another frontage road, old Highway 6, to reach Heaton Bay Campground on Dillon Reservoir. This section of the ride is a part of the Trans-American Bicycle Route. If you want details about this route, write to Bikecentennial at P.O. Box 8308, Missoula, Montana 59807.

Gore Pass turned out to be one of the most delightful passes we rode anywhere. We met very little traffic, and a gradual grade to the summit. There are 3 campgrounds along this route: Tonopas Creek located at the top of the first long hill; Black Tail further up; and Gore Pass Campground located on the summit.

From Tonopas over Gore Pass to the intersection with Highway 40 outside Kremmling are 27 totally enjoyable miles. However, upon reaching Highway 40 again, you will have 6 miles of heavy traffic to contend with once again as you ride back to Kremmling.

From Kremmling, you have another choice to make: either cross over Loveland Pass or Berthoud Pass. Loveland is slightly higher at 11,992 feet, while Berthoud's summit is 11,314 feet. If you select Loveland Pass, follow Highway 9 into Silverthorne where you'll pass another campground: Blue River Campground, 8 miles north of Silverthorne.

To cross Loveland Pass from Dillon, continue east on Highway 6, passing the Snake River Saloon and the Keystone Ski area with lodging and food. The climb of 8 miles is 2836 feet from Dillon to the top of the pass, and should only be made when the weather is what local pilots call "severe clear." You definitely don't want to be on top should there be a thunderstorm in the area.

After coming off the top and meeting I-70, ride along the shoulder of the Interstate for 5 miles, taking Exit 221 to Bakerville. Now follow the asphalt frontage road along Clear Creek down to Silver Plume where you once again return to the shoulder of the Interstate to ride 5 miles into Georgetown.

While in Georgetown, you might want to overnight at the

Alpine Inn Lodge (569-3211); Swiss Inn (869-2931); or the Georgetown Motor Inn (569-3201).

Places to eat include the Swiss Inn, Whiffletree, Los Dos Mujeres, and the Old Chicago Spaghetti and Pizza Company.

This very picturesque, historic old mining town also offers some good sightseeing such as the old Hamill House constructed in 1880, the Hotel de Paris, and the Georgetown-Silver Plume train ride. This ride is well worth the time just to see the famous Georgetown Loop where the tracks loop back on themselves several times to climb back out of the valley for 600 feet before continuing on to Silver Plume where you can purchase a snack at the Plume Saloon every day except Mondays.

From Georgetown, you continue along the frontage road all the way to Idaho Springs, 12.4 miles away. Just imagine: this road is used for a foot race in mid-August. Aren't you glad you're coasting down it on your bicycle?

Once in Idaho Springs, home of another hot springs pool and restaurant/hotel, you may wish to visit the old Argo Mine. This is the world's longest mining tunnel, traversing 5 miles underground to Central City.

Places to stay in Idaho Springs include: Argo Motor Inn (567-4473); Blair Motel (567-2077); Hanson Lodge (567-2838); and Krenzel Motel (567-2492).

Good eating is found at Beau Jo's, the Golddigger Restaurant, Sandwich Mines, the 6 and 40 Restaurant, or at the Sugar Plum.

From Idaho Springs, cross over the Interstate and again follow the frontage road. You will encounter a short stretch of dirt one mile long, but then you're back onto asphalt again.

Continue along this frontage road until you rejoin the Interstate at Exit 243 for 1 mile. At the next intersection that you see on your left going to Golden via Clear Creek Canyon, you must cross 2 lanes of traffic to get off the Interstate and onto Highway 6 since bicycles aren't permitted on the Interstate at this point. Use extreme care here in crossing the highway!

Ride a very short distance, .8 mile, to the second turn-off for Floyd Hill. Bicycles are prohibited along Highway 6, so you must exit this highway onto Floyd Hill. Climb up the hill and continue to follow Highway 40 for another 4 miles before crossing over to the south side of I-70. Follow the frontage road until reaching the El Rancho, a good place to get some great cinnamon rolls, and then get back onto the right-hand shoulder of I-70 for 2 more miles. Exit at 254: Genessee Park. Cross over the Interstate and follow Highway 40 the rest of the way down Mt. Vernon Canyon, another 6 miles.

From here, to return to Boulder, upon reaching the traffic light at the bottom of the hill, turn left and cycle a short distance, passing the Heidelberg Restaurant. Turn left onto Highway 93 a short distance later below Heritage Square.

Follow Highway 93 a short distance further to Highway 6. Turn left at the traffic light and cycle west to the next traffic light outside of Golden.

At this next light, turn right and cycle to Washington Avenue. Turn left again and follow Washington through town where it becomes Highway 93 again, the most direct route to Boulder.

Golden has 2 bike shops along Washington Avenue: Golden Bicycle Works at 12th and Washington, and the Pack 'N Pedal Shop at 11th and Washington.

Highway 93 is heavily traveled by trucks, particularly the stretch just outside of Golden, and has no shoulder for cyclists with the exception of a 1 mile stretch of bike path, so extreme caution should be exercised.

To avoid some of this heavy traffic, you might prefer to take what the locals refer to as the "Back Door" route, which only adds a few miles to your ride. From Washington Avenue in Golden, cycle north to 10th Avenue which is by the large city park in the south end of town. Turn right on 10th and cycle east to either McIntyre Street or Easley Road where you turn left in either case. Either route leads to West 64th Avenue where you turn right to ride a short distance to Highway 72. Turn left.

After going under a bridge, take the right fork for Indiana Avenue which goes to the north. This road narrows and becomes very hilly, terminating at Highway 128 at the top of the longest hill. From here, turn left, and for the shortest route to town, turn right at the next intersection on McCaslin Blvd. to cycle down the well-known hills of the Morgul Bismarck ridden in the Coors Classic Bike Race: the Hump and the Wall.

93

After passing the small town of Superior at the bottom of the second hill, turn west onto Marshall Drive. Follow this newly paved country road to Highway 93. The road will swing southwest bypassing the old coal mining town of Marshall, whose main street I generally avoid because of its poor condition.

At Highway 93, turn right and continue 2 more miles into Boulder.

Meanwhile back in Kremmling, if you have chosen to cycle over Berthoud Pass, you'll climb from 7955 feet to 11,314 feet. Along this route, you'll pass a campground at Tabernash and ride into Winter Park. Here you'll find many motels and places to snack as well as a bike shop in the Park Plaza Center.

For a ski lift ride to the top of one of the ski lifts, Mary Jane, why not stop on the south side of town? You'll get another chance for a lift ride upon reaching the top of Berthoud Pass.

The ride up Berthoud Pass begins as a fairly flat ride but then it begins to climb quite steadily once you go around the first long switchback. However, you'll have a nice wide shoulder all the way. Once on top you can either buy a snack in their cafe or eat your own lunch at one of the picnic tables located on the rooftop of the cafe.

The coast down Berthoud is not along a shoulder until you're in Berthoud Falls. However, when ridden at mid-day during the week, we encountered very light traffic, all of which gave us plenty of room as we swung around the hairpin curves coming off the top.

As you pass through Empire, you might wish to stop for a snack at the Peck Hotel, first established in 1860 and which is now one of the oldest hotels in the state. Empire was also an early gold camp which was used by the Ute Indians as a stopping point as they passed by on their way to trade in Denver.

At the bottom of the pass, you'll connect with the frontage road along the south side of I-70 below Georgetown. Now you can proceed as described earlier for the route over Loveland Pass.

Bibliography

Trail Guides, Aspen, by Raymond Auger et al.
Tour Book, Southwestern, AAA.
The New Aspen Area Trail Guide, Michael O'Shea, 1975.
Woodall's Campground Directory, 1979 Western Edition,
    Woodall Publishing Co., Illinois.
Campground Guide for Tent and Trailer Tourists, Campgrounds,
    Unlimited, Wakefield, Kansas.
Unique Ghost Towns and Mountain Spots, Caroline Bancroft,
    Johnson Publishing Co., Boulder, 1971.
Where to Vacation in CO, AAA.
Jeep Trails to Colorado Ghost Towns, Robert L. Brown, Caxton
    Printers, Ltd., Caldwell, Idaho, 1972.
Tales, Trails and Tommyknockers, Myriam Friggens, Johnson
    Publishing Co., 1979.
Western Yesterdays, Forest Crossen, Boulder Publishing Co.
"Coming 'Round the Mountain on Georgetown's famous
    loop," Boulder Daily *Camera* Focus, June 22, 1980.
"Black Canyon of the Gunnison," National Park Service.
Greenhorn Guide, CO's Gold Circle, Special edition Clear
    Creek Courant, Idaho Springs, CO.
"Idaho Springs looks exactly like a post card," Focus, July 6,
    1980.
Colorado Accommodations Guide, Convention and Visitor's
    Bureau.
A Climbing Guide to Colorado's Fourteeners, Walter Borneman
    and Lyndon Lampert, Pruett Publishing, 1979.

Numerous pamphlets from throughout the state obtained
    from various chambers of commerce.

To obtain bicycling strip maps of the state, contact the Department of Highways, Division Transportation and Planning, 4201 E. Arkansas Ave., Denver
80222. Attention: Bill Litchfield. Note: These maps are $1.50 per packet, and
there are 4 different routes (packets) from which to choose.